A GUIDE FOR PERSONAL FINANCES

Merlon Harper

ISBN: 978-1-4834-3453-7 (sc)
ISBN: 978-1-4834-3455-1 (hc)
ISBN: 978-1-4834-3454-4 (e)

Library of Congress Control Number: 2015910929

Lulu Publishing Services rev. date: 10/21/2015

CONTENTS

DEDICATION

I'm dedicating *Financial Freedom* to my mother; she was the first person to expose me to valuable financial concepts that have served me well. In her own way and in her own lingo, she taught me how to master the five elements of the FICO credit score. She always said, "Pay your bills on time, and you will always get credit." She was a master at manipulating and leveraging credit to her benefit; she had to be in order to keep her family of nine fed and clothed after my father died. All the retailers in our town were ready and willing to offer her credit. I understood later that it was because she didn't pose a risk to them; she always met her obligations in a timely manner. I'm amazed at how she calculated and strategized financial moves, ensuring that she was never overextended. Thanks, Mom; you are my inspiration and my idol.

I also want to thank my husband, who encouraged me to write this book. He understands how crucial early financial literacy is and how important it was for me to write *Financial Freedom*. I want to thank my children, Lawrence and Keallah, they provided me with the canvas for *Financial Freedom*.

FOREWORD

Financial literacy is critical early in life, as it helps us develop a certain mind-set that will last a lifetime. We tend to prepare for the workforce but not for the financial world. However, everyone should understand important financial concepts for the complex world we live in; everyone should have a solid foundation in finance in order to think critically, weigh risks, and make informed financial decisions.

Personal finance, as the name implies, is often considered personal and, therefore, is not always something parents share with their children. We don't want to share the burden of finances with our children, because we want to shelter them from the complicated world of finance.

There are programs that teach children to open bank accounts and save their allowances, but little attention is devoted to explaining financial outcomes of actions or inaction. *Financial Freedom* provides information and examples that will allow you to analyze information so that you may grasp the larger conceptual context of finance and gain a greater understanding of the financial world.

There are countless adults who are able to make living wages but don't understand the relationship between their FICO scores and renting an apartment, owning a home, or paying more for credit. So many are— or will become—unbanked or underbanked, always paying more for goods and services because they don't understand the consequences of mishandling a checking account or a low credit score. What you don't know *can* hurt you. *Financial Freedom* can help you build wealth, make informed financial decisions, and thrive in our free-enterprise system.

INTRODUCTION

Everyone will become a consumer at some point in his or her life, and almost everyone will need to make some financial decisions, but often we aren't prepared. Consumer actions and financial decisions have major impacts on our lives. If you make bad decisions, you may become a statistic, part of the millions of Americans who are deeply in debt, underbanked, and undersaved, with a thwarted road to achieving financial freedom and your American dream.

We can all benefit from understanding personal finance; it can provide extra armor against unscrupulous business practices and prepare us to survive and thrive in our free-enterprise system. Whether you are a millionaire businessperson or a secretary earning $30,000 a year, personal-finance knowledge can help you reduce your debt, build wealth, and know your consumer rights and options.

Unfortunately, financial management is often limited or left off the school curriculum. Considering the estimated billions in interest and fees paid in 2013 by millions of underbanked and unbanked Americans, personal finance should be a required subject in every school. Check-cashing and similar companies have created a profitable market, easily dangling attractive bait to the underbanked, taking advantage of their positions. Similar in fashion, car-title loans cost the undersaved consumer an estimated $3.6 billion a year in interest generated from $1.6 billion in loans; that's $2 billion in gross profits. As of 2013, twenty-six states continue to allow predatory lending practices, despite the fact it derails the economic security of vulnerable Americans. Predatory lending is defined by the Federal Deposit Insurance Corporation as "imposing unfair and abusive loan terms on borrowers."

Payday loans operate under a similar premise, with companies charging 300 percent or more in interest—in 2012, profits from payday loans amounted to approximately $45 billion. An alarming statistic for 2015 shows the average American household credit card debt at $15,609. A 2013 survey conducted by Bankrate.com found that 27 percent of Americans had no emergency savings, essentially living from paycheck to paycheck. Fifty-eight percent of preretirees don't have a retirement plan, and those near retirement have an average of only $25,000 saved, barely enough to support them through one year of retirement. Most Americans will become taxpayers but find the law too complex to prepare their tax returns. They may turn to unscrupulous tax-return preparers or make costly tax decisions, leaving them with large debts that force them to wait years to retire.

Obtaining a good post–high school education or skill certainly has the potential to propel you into a good financial status. Without a skill or education, it may be difficult to financially succeed. Unskilled-labor jobs have been declining in the United States for years; more companies are outsourcing unskilled jobs to other countries because it's cheaper and increases their bottom lines.

It has been said that the amount of wealth you can accumulate is directly linked to your education and career decisions. This is true to a large extent; the more education you have, the more you can expect in salary, and some careers pay more money than others. So think about your career choices, and challenge yourself by investing in your future and future earnings.

According to the National Center for Education Statistics, without a high-school education, you can expect to earn a median salary of about $23,900, not enough to support a family in a middle-class lifestyle. The median salary with a high-school diploma is about $30,000; with an associate degree, $37,500; and a bachelor's degree, $48,500. A master's degree can hit the mark of $59,600. Professional degrees can command even more.

But don't let the cost of your education take you off the path of financial freedom. It could mean the difference between surviving and being financially free. Most graduates don't fully understand the gravity of student-loan debt on their futures. In 2013, there were approximately forty million Americans with a combined student-loan debt of $1.2 trillion. A student loan can impact your life for years. Some borrowers have obligations for as long as thirty years. Senator Marco Rubio owed more than $100,000 in student loans when he was sworn into office in January 2011, and President Barack Obama retired his student-loan debt just before his election as the forty-fourth president of the United States.

Borrowers can't charge off or eliminate student-loan debt in bankruptcy, and wages can be garnished for payments. President Obama recognized the burden student loans carry, so he decided to move forward with a plan in 2014 to introduce policy aimed at easing the burden for millions of new student-loan borrowers. His proposal limits the maximum payment to 10 percent of the borrower's income and the ability to discharge unpaid debt after twenty years—or after ten years, if they provide certain government services.

Consumer expert Clark Howard has a rule of thumb; that is, you should not borrow more for a four-year degree than the entry-level salary you expect to make. There are other ways you can get a degree without long-term debt:

- Consider two years of community college before entering a four-year college; it's cheaper.
- Pay as you go; work part-time to pay your tuition or a portion of it.
- Apply for scholarships—athletic, academic, and so forth.
- Finish your matriculation early to eliminate the cost of additional semester expenses.
- Decide early which field of study you wish to pursue, avoiding a costly program change.

Making a ton of money doesn't necessarily equate to building wealth; it's only one factor. Take the rapper M. C. Hammer, who coined the phrase "Can't touch this." He earned $33 million in 1990 and declared bankruptcy in 1996 with $13.7 million in debts. In the same year, film star Burt Reynolds filed for bankruptcy. In 2003 Mike Tyson, the notorious professional boxer and the youngest to win and hold the title of heavyweight champion, earned over $300 million but filed for bankruptcy after being in debt for $23 million.

While education choices and career decisions can certainly afford you the ability to amass large sums of money, financial knowledge and a good financial strategy can help you keep it and produce more.

Test your knowledge

What are the names of the three major credit bureaus?

What does a credit score determine?

What are the five elements of a credit score?

What is the highest credit score you can obtain?

What score ensures you of getting the best available rate?

Do you know anyone with an 850 credit score?

How safe are your bank deposits?

Why should you save money?

What is the ChexSystems?

What documents do you need to open a bank account?

What are some of the benefits of a banking account?

What do you need to rent an apartment?

What do you need to purchase a home?

What information do you need before purchasing a vehicle?

How much does a car depreciate each year?

Name three investment vehicles.

Are gifts you receive taxable?

Why do you need retirement income?

Do you need a will?

What is a revocable trust?

What type of insurance do you need, and how much?

CHAPTER 1

Money and Banking

After you have prepared for and entered into your career of choice and begin to earn money, you will need a safe place to manage it; having a bank account can help. Your deposits are secure up to $250,000 for each account—checking, savings, money market, and the like. Bank accounts are beneficial in so many ways—they are a secure place to deposit your payroll checks, pay bills, save, and handle other financial transactions.

When opening accounts, choose your financial institution carefully to ensure it meets your needs and to avoid costly, unnecessary banking expenses. Consider the monthly fees, interest rates, minimum balance requirements, per-check charges, location, ATM locations, options for direct deposit, and overall banking services. If you choose the wrong bank, you may be nickeled and dimed to the poor house. Take, for example, a free checking account offered at a major bank that will charge five dollars a month for its "free" account if you don't make a minimum of ten transactions per month. It's important to read the fine print.

Some banks charge as much as $10 a month for maintenance fees; that's $120 a year. If you invested $120 every year in the stock market for twenty years with an average return of 10 percent, you would have over $7,500. If the bank used your $120 and $120 from a total of twenty thousand customers and invested it at the same rate at the beginning of each of the twenty years, it will earn $151,205,998. Now you can understand the incentive to charge you fees. Many banks waive their maintenance fee if certain conditions are met—for example, maintaining a certain balance. If ten thousand of the twenty thousand bank customers maintain a $1,000 balance, the bank can make short-term investments or loans from your deposits to earn similar revenue. Yes, it's a win-win situation for the bank, but you can be a winner too by making good choices. Most credit unions don't charge a monthly fee, making them a viable alternative to traditional banks.

An overdraft charge is another expensive fee that can create an additional debt for you in the form of a negative balance. An overdraft occurs when you don't have enough money in your account to cover transactions you have made—from check writing, debit card purchases, or cash withdrawals from ATMs. You can opt to have overdraft protection, but that can be expensive as well.

Sometimes overdrafts occur because banking customers don't keep an account of their balance in relation to the amount spent, which is simply careless. Another reason is that the customer may assume a deposit will be credited on a specific day when, in fact, there may be a two- or three-day hold before funds are available. Sometimes customers take a gamble by making a transaction and hoping it's not presented to the bank for payment before a future deposit is credited, another risky strategy. Sometimes banks manipulate the timing of deposits and payments to give the customer the best chance of creating an overdraft. Overdraft fees can range from twenty to thirty-five dollars, a flat rate the bank charges to loan money to cover a customer's insufficiently funded transaction.

To demonstrate how overdrafts are created, take, for example, a check payment to a retail store. When the check reaches the bank for thirty dollars, you have insufficient funds to cover it. The bank covers the payment and charges you thirty-three dollars in overdraft fees. Thirty-three dollars for a thirty-dollar payment equates to a 1,000 percent annual percentage rate. Ouch! In addition to the fee, you are also responsible for the amount the bank covered, thirty dollars. This can create a domino effect; each additional check presented to the bank on your behalf for payment will get the same treatment until you deposit sufficient funds or the bank closes your account.

My nephew Larry graduated from high school in 2008, landed a job, and opened a new checking account in his neighborhood. The bank offered him a debit card for withdrawing money from the ATM and to make purchases. Larry had his paycheck automatically deposited to his checking account and rarely wrote checks. He received a welcome package from the bank when he opened the account, but he never read it. He didn't keep records of his transactions either. At any given time, Larry was unaware of exactly how much money he had available to spend, so he continued to use his debit card for cash and purchases and assumed that the bank would contact him if there was a problem.

There was a problem: Larry had overdrawn his account by $105 with his last four small-dollar transactions, which ended up costing him an additional $120 (four $30 overdraft fees). Larry was stunned by the exorbitant fees and was unable to pay them. His next paycheck covered the overdraft and the fees but left him unable to pay his regular expenses. Larry was never able to catch up and eventually closed the account, frustrated with the process. Larry is currently unbanked, which is also expensive and hinders his quest for financial freedom.

The new overdraft rules created in 2010 could have benefited Larry. They basically require the bank to provide you with the choice to opt in or out of overdraft protection and not automatically enroll you in the plan and charge you fees. Under the new rules, Larry could have opted out of the overdraft protection that the bank offered, and his insufficient funds transactions would have been declined by the bank, and he would not have had those crippling fees.

The new rules don't apply to checks and automatic bill payment, so your bank may sign you up for overdraft protections, and you may not have a choice to opt out in these situations. Talk to your banker to determine your bank's policy; if you have a tight budget, careful monitoring and management becomes crucial. If you close your account and fail to pay the fees, you may end up on the ChexSystems.

ChexSystems

You may find yourself on the ChexSystems if you defaulted on a bank account, had insufficient funds unpaid, wrote bad checks, or were part of illegal banking activities. Keep in mind that you can't spend more than you have in your account without consequences. ChexSystems maintains and reports consumers' negative banking history. Once a banking institution reports you to the ChexSystems, you can remain there for five years even if you pay the debt and fees in full. Some banks only rely on this report, so as long as you have a good check-writing history, your bad credit may not be a factor; other banks may require both a good check-writing history and a good credit history.

Some banks offer an opportunity for a second chance. For example, Wells Fargo Bank offers the Opportunity Checking Account, specifically for individuals who have been reported to the ChexSystems and are struggling to open an account. Be aware that they have their restrictions and regulations, and they may cost you more to maintain than a traditional bank account. Very few banks, if any, will allow you to open an account outside of the five-year window if you were involved in any illegal banking activities.

If, unfortunately, you find yourself on the ChexSystems, you can obtain a copy of your report at https://www.consumerdebit.com/consumerinfo/us/es/chexsystems/report/index.htm. The report, similar to a credit report, will include your personal identifiable information, including any aliases you have used or previous addresses. Anyone who pulls your report will also find the name of the bank that reported you, the date reported, the reason why, the amount charged off, and so on. Ideally you want to have good credit and a good banking history. You don't want to be unbanked or underbanked, as you will find yourself paying higher fees and often inconvenienced, not to mention thwarted on the road to building wealth.

Banking has become a risky business for banks; sometimes they lose money covering bad checks and advancing payments for insufficient account holders, so a few of the big banks came together to create another check-verification service that's gaining popularity called "Early Warning Service," an extra layer of protection for the banks and another hurdle for you.

When faced with a tough situation, it becomes increasingly easy to fall prey to Internet sites that promise to remove you from the ChexSystems for a fee. You can be scammed, with no results. Remember, you can obtain your own report for free. If any mistakes are on the report, you can correct them yourself for free. If the report is accurate, you may contact the reporting bank yourself to determine if there are certain conditions that you can meet to have them remove your name; otherwise, you will need to wait the five years or find alternative banking.

You should open a bank account only when you are able to manage it responsibly. You'll need a few things to open one: personal identification (driver's license, learner's permit, state ID card, passport, military ID, or school ID), a mailing address, contact phone number, Social Security number, and a good check-writing and credit history. The bank or credit union will check your credit history with the credit bureaus and/or your check-writing history with the ChexSystems.

Online Banking

Online banking is so convenient; you can avoid making trips to the bank or buying postage stamps and envelopes. An example of a true online bank is Ally. To become a member of this bank you will need a high credit score and cannot be on the ChexSystems, because they check both. Brick-and-mortar buildings do not exist for this bank—transactions are handled online offering the same services as traditional banks, and usually you can expect to earn higher interest rates on accounts.

Alternatively, you can choose a brick-and-mortar bank and take advantage of its online banking services. You can have your paychecks directly deposited, and other checks can be scanned in using a smartphone and other devices. You can use your debit card to pay for purchases instead of writing a check. Some debtors offer a discount for online paper statements and automatic drafts from your account. Other advantages include the ability to review statements online, easily transfer money between accounts, and view balances on most Internet-connected devices. A major advantage brick-and-mortar banks have over true online banking is the option of speaking with someone in person at your local branch for problem resolution. The disadvantage is usually lower rates of return on your accounts; the person who solves your problem has to be paid on a continued basis.

Just select your bank and follow the instructions from the bank for setting up and using online banking. You can set up automatic payments and avoid ever being late on a payment for recurring fixed payments. Nonfixed payments require one or two more steps.

Online banking tends to be a bit easier to balance because most transactions are instant or pending to your account. However, it is still a good idea to keep your receipts for purchases to compare the amount of the expenditure to the amount that appears on your account. Once I attended a popular comedy club in Atlanta for a show and dinner with a few friends. I paid with my debit card, adding a 15 percent tip to the total bill. A few days later, I reviewed the charges to my checking account online and noticed an unusual charge. The five-dollar tip I'd left the waitress had been converted to twenty-five dollars. I was appalled over the blatant disregard for my money, so I immediately contacted my bank to resolve the discrepancy. Fortunately for me, I had retained the original receipt and was able to verify the correct charges. The bank immediately reversed the charges; however, if I didn't have the receipt to prove the charges, I would have paid the extra twenty dollars. Also, keep a record of those rare checks your write; they don't always appear instantly.

Whether you use traditional banking, online banking, or a combination, you should balance your account each month. Record in your check register each transaction, including deposits, debits, and checks written. Once you receive your statement, record items that appear on the monthly statement received from the bank that were not previously recorded in the check register. Add any deposits or credits and subtract any checks or debits made since the date of the statement. If you are unable to reconcile your statement, you may need to refer back to your last month's statement. If unable to reconcile the statement after referring back and checking the math, contact your banking institution to report errors.

CHAPTER 2

Building Wealth with a Higher Credit Score

Credit Score Ratings	
Credit Score	Description
760 – 849	Excellent
700 – 759	Great
660 – 699	Good
620 – 659	Average
580 – 619	Poor
below 579	Very Poor

The first wealth-building rule of thumb is to live below your means. This means that you should be able to pay your bills comfortably with discretionary funds for saving and investing. Second, avoid paying more for credit and services by maintaining a good credit score. A person with a credit score of 780 is going to pay less for credit than one with a 620 rating. Your credit score is a snapshot of where you stand today; this means that you can change it over a period of time. Poor credit today can be good credit tomorrow, but the pendulum swings both ways.

Fico Score

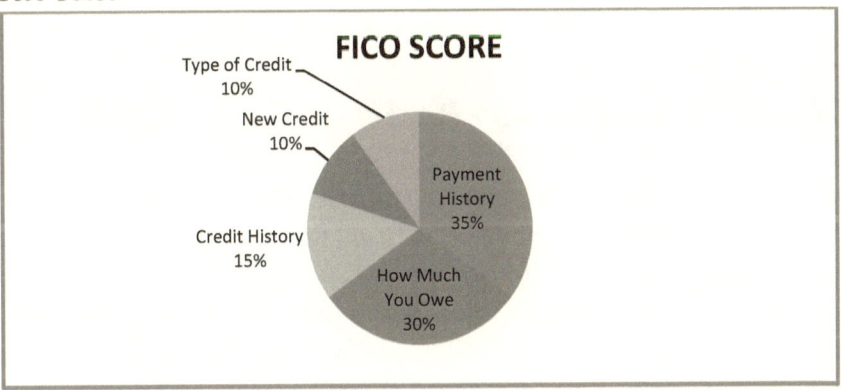

FICO scores can range from 300 to 850. The three-digit number and its five components are used to determine if you are approved for credit and at what interest rate—whether it's a credit card, car loan, or a mortgage. It's your financial passport to everything with a credit component. FICO is short for Fair Isaac Company; lenders use these scores to evaluate their risk of lending you money. The higher the score, the more favorable your interest rate will be. If you haven't reached the maximum score of 850 yet, you are not alone. If you are a member of the elite 800 club, that's great however, once you reach a score of 780, you should be offered the best rates available.

Payment History—35 Percent

Thirty-five percent of your FICO score is attributable to your payment history. The largest portion of your credit score depends on you paying your bills on time. However, it's a little more complicated than that. Apparently, the diversity of the accounts you pay on time is important too. Examples of diverse accounts include credit cards (Visa, MasterCard, Discover, and American Express), retail accounts (department store credit cards), and installment loans (mortgage loans, car loans, etc.).

Negative items in this category include late payments over thirty days, bankruptcy, foreclosures, liens, judgments, and other collection activities. Don't fret; time softens the blows of those negatives.

How Much You Owe—30 Percent

This section is your debt-to-credit ratio. It's the second-largest part of your credit score, consisting of 30 percent. To put it simply, it is how much you owe compared to how much credit you have. It too can be complex; let's say you opened your first credit account with a limit of $500 and create $350 in debt. Your debt-to-credit ratio is 70 percent. Seventy percent is too high; your credit score does not favor these circumstances. To lenders, it appears that you will soon max out your credit card, and it could indicate that you are overextended and more likely to make some payments late or not at all.

This score takes into account the amount you owe on all accounts. If you have two credit cards with a combined limit of $3,000 and total debt of $350, your ratio would decrease to 12 percent, a great ratio and a positive in this category.

In this category the FICO score takes into account the amount you owe on different types of accounts as well. High revolving credit balances have more of a negative impact than high installment-loan balances. Revolving credit, such as a department store card or a regular credit card, affords you continuous use and the chance to max out at any time. On the other hand, an installment loan, such as a mortgage or car loan, does not provide easy access to your available credit, so timely payments with higher debt than credit doesn't appear to be a negative on this type of debt. Actually, in some cases, a mortgage will improve your credit score. This does not mean that you should run out and get a mortgage before you are ready. This doesn't mean that you shouldn't have a credit card either; depending on other factors and circumstances, a person with a well-managed credit card will have a better score than someone without one at all.

Having balances on a large number of accounts concurrently, however small, creates an appearance to the lender that you may be overextended, displaying the need to spread debt without the ability to pay recurring expenses. Closing accounts with zero balances is not a good idea; it will not only increase the percent of accounts with balances but also increase your debt-to credit ratio. Both situations have the potential to lower your score.

Credit History—15 Percent

You just read about two good reasons for not closing credit, and there are more. The length of credit matters to your score; a longer credit history can increase your score. Once you close an account, you can also lose the account history. You have probably heard that you shouldn't open up excessive new accounts in a short period of time. Why? Because your credit score takes into account your oldest account, your newest account, and the average age of all your accounts. All things considered, new accounts bring down the average age of accounts. But remember that the credit score is a snapshot in time; those new accounts will eventually become old accounts, providing you don't consistently open new accounts. Also remember that the mere fact of opening a new account has the potential to lower your credit score.

New Credit—10 Percent

In this category, your FICO score is affected by the amount of new credit, sorted by type and how often you open new credit. You probably know this category by how inquiries affect your score. When you apply for a new account, someone probably inquired about your credit. Inquiries remain on your credit report for two years, but only the last twelve months are considered. Some inquires, although reported, don't affect your risk and are not counted, like an employer checking your credit for employment.

Rate shopping for mortgages and cars made within a set period of time only counts as one inquiry against your score. An additional inquiry could cost you less than five points, but many inquiries can cost you more points. More inquiries have been shown to increase your risk for bankruptcy. The length of your credit is a factor in considering inquiries.

Type of Credit—10 Percent

This section considers your mix of credit. Does your credit portfolio only consist of credit cards, or is it a mix of installment loans, credit cards, retail accounts, and mortgage loans? The total number of accounts in a specific category matters. It can be a negative to have a myriad of accounts with subprime lenders. You could perform all positive actions in each of the categories but still be unable to achieve the perfect score. This could be because of subprime lenders, since the type of credit represents 10 percent of your score. You may have a subprime lender if you ever applied for instant credit at a retail store when the retailer offered you a chance to save 15 percent today and earn points later by applying for credit right now. Approving instant credit is a risk for lenders; they are taking a chance on you, and, therefore, you pay the price with subprime interest rates, usually over 20 percent.

You are entitled to a free report each year under the Fair Credit Reporting Act; you are also entitled to a free report within sixty days of being turned down by a lender if it was based on your credit score. Use this information to correct any errors or to protect yourself from identity theft. A free credit report under the Fair Credit Reporting Act can be obtained online at https://www.annualcreditreport.com/index.action or by calling 1-877-322-8228 or mailing an Annual Credit Report Request Form to Annual Credit Report Request Service, PO Box 105281, Atlanta, GA 30348-5281. Don't contact the credit bureaus directly; they only provide free reports using the contact information above. Don't get scammed by anyone claiming they can get your free credit report; again, the request is only through annualcreditreport.com, 1-877-322-8228, or mail to Annual Credit Report Request Service.

In order to obtain your report, you will be asked to provide your name, address, Social Security number, and date of birth. In addition, you will be asked security questions that only you would know the answer to. For example, you may be asked to identify a previous residence from a list of addresses. Acquiring your credit report online is usually instant; the other two methods may take as much as two weeks.

You should order your credit reports annually or stagger them by ordering one each quarter. Reviewing your credit report can help you get a jump on any potential identity theft, identify errors, and analyze your accounts, including your mix of credit.

Dispute credit report errors at http://www.consumer.ftc.gov/articles/0151 -disputing-errors-credit-reports.

The three major credit bureaus and their contact information are listed below:

Credit Bureau	Phone Number	Website
Equifax	800-685-1111	www.equifax.com
Experian	888-397-3742	www.experian.com
TransUnion	800-916-8800	www.transunion.com

You may find yourself soliciting the help of a credit-repair agency when your score entitles you to no credit or subprime predatory rates. Before you do, remember that you can be more effective in repairing your own credit than any agency, minus the fees.

Although the pie chart above gives you a percentage value for each category, exactly how many points you'll gain or lose for taking a specific action is not exact. The scoring model is proprietary information; however, there is evidence that there is a range of point deductions for certain actions. In addition, the higher your credit score, the more credit mistakes will affect it.

The Credit Effect

Credit Mistake	If your score is 680	If your score is 780
Maxed-out card	Down 10 to 30 points	Down 25 to 45 points
Thirty-day late payment	Down 60 to 80 points	Down 90 to 110 points
Debt settlement	Down 45 to 65 points	Down 105 to 125 points
Foreclosure	Down 85 to 105 points	Down 140 to 160 points
Bankruptcy	Down 130 to 150 points	Down 220 to 240 points

Source: FICO

Let's just say that you made one of the five credit mistakes; in most cases, negative dings remain on your credit report for seven years, ten years for bankruptcy. If for whatever reason you don't pay a debt, do you know how long a creditor has to collect the unpaid debt? It's different throughout the states; some are clearly defined, and others are ambiguous at best. The statute of limitations is usually between three and ten years depending on the type of debt; for court judgments, it can be as long as twenty years.

Let's say your state has a six-year statute of limitations to collect a debt on an open-ended account before it's time-barred. After the statute of limitations is over, the creditor can continue to try collecting the account, but they cannot legally make you pay in court. This is assuming that you respond to any court order served requesting you to respond or appear in court. You can use this opportunity to dispute the debt or prove that the time limit to collect has expired. If you are unsure of whether your debt has expired, you can ask the collector, who is obligated to answer truthfully. If they refuse to answer, you can send a certified letter requesting proof of the debt and how they calculated the statute of limitations. Making a payment can reage the account, and sometimes just acknowledging an old debt reages it.

It's a mistake to ignore your debts; if a creditor files a judgment against you in court, it will appear on your credit report as a negative and can remain on your report for as long as seven years, whether paid or unpaid. Some states allow the renewal of judgments after the initial one expires two or more times; you may never improve your credit score. In addition, your wages may be garnished, your bank account frozen, or a lien placed on your property.

The statute of limitations usually begins on an open-ended account from the day the debt or payment was due. Read the clauses in the agreement; some creditors say that the statute does not begin until they make a demand for payment or until some other act occurs. You can check the statute of limitations in your state with a legal aid lawyer or your state's attorney general.

Statutes of limitations apply differently to these debts:

- oral agreement—agreement made verbally and/or with a handshake
- written agreement—a signed document agreeing to pay a debt
- promissory note—a signed document agreeing to pay scheduled payments
- open-ended account—an account with varying balances open to new charges, such as a credit card

It helps if you understand how credit works and how it affects your life. Credit scores are a snapshot of your risk at a particular time, which is why it is possible to change your credit score. Increasing your credit score is like losing weight. It takes time and discipline, and the longer you do nothing, the longer it takes. Also, like losing weight, it takes active management to maintain.

Creditors may change the guidelines of their risk evaluations based on the economy and other factors. Interest rates also fluctuate due to some of the same factors. The chart below from *Money Magazine* shows approval and interest rates for various types of loans broken down by credit score for the year 2010, shortly after the mortgage crisis and the tanking of the economy. It was not only hard to get approval, but the rates were higher.

Credit Score	Loan Type	Rate
500	Auto loan approval	19%
620	Mortgage approval	5.9%
660	Credit card approval	20%
720	Best auto loan rate	5.3%
740	Best credit card rate	7.5%
760–850	Best mortgage rate	4.3%

Money Magazine September 2010, "The Quest for the Perfect Credit Score"

Vechicle Loan Example

Purchase Price	Term	Interest Rate	Credit Score	Payment
$20,000	5 yrs.	19%	585	$518.81
$20,000	5 yrs.	5.3%	720	**$380.18**

With a 720 credit score for the same term at a more favorable interest rate, you can save $138.63 a month and $8,317.80 over the five-year term.

Credit Card Balance Example

Balance	Term	Interest Rate	Credit Score	Payment
$5,000	**5 yrs. (open-ended)**	**18%**	**660**	**$150.00**

It will take forty-seven months to retire the credit card debt with the minimum payment of $150, assuming you don't accumulate any new debt, and you will pay $2,050 in interest. Using the same example, with a credit score of 740 and thus a more favorable rate of 7.5 percent, a payment of $150 will enable you to retire the debt in thirty-two months.

You can achieve these same results with the 18 percent interest rate by paying just $50 more each month ($200), retiring the debt in thirty-two months and paying only $1,541 in interest. Although your credit score may be low, which bridles you with a high interest rate, you can get out of debt sooner by making extra payments; your credit card statements disclose this information thanks to the credit card reform law of 2009. Paying more coupled with paying on time can improve your credit score, qualifying you for a more favorable interest rate in the future.

Exercise

Compute the mortgage principal and interest payment for the two scenarios using the following information.

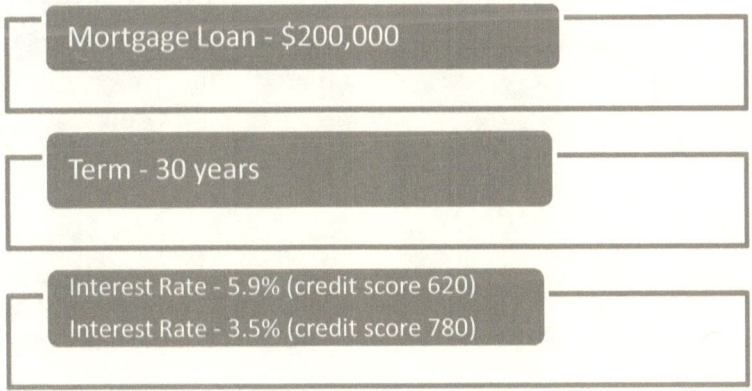

Mortgage Loan - $200,000

Term - 30 years

Interest Rate - 5.9% (credit score 620)
Interest Rate - 3.5% (credit score 780)

Answer: $1,180 and $895, respectively. A higher credit score allows you to have $285 extra each month for the same loan amount.

Increase Your Credit Score

There are strategies you can use to help increase and maintain a good credit score so that you can pay less for a vehicle, credit card, or mortgage and have more money for saving, investing, and building wealth.

- Order your free credit report each year from the three credit bureaus: Equifax, Experian, and TransUnion. You can order your credit score for about twenty dollars or less. Keep in mind that credit reports may not be identical; some businesses report to all three bureaus, and others do not. The credit bureaus may also use different scoring models, which will affect your score.

When applying for credit, the creditor will likely use the middle score from the three bureaus to extend credit. If a husband and wife both apply for a mortgage loan and one spouse has a good credit score while the other has a lower credit score, the middle score of the spouse with the lowest credit score will be used. Consequently, they may not qualify for the best rate jointly.

Spouse 1		
Experian 801	Equifax 792	Trans Union 798

Spouse 2		
Experian 650	Trans Union 635	Equifax 645

- Pay your accounts on time. Making payments on time is a major factor in the most critical section of your credit report—payment history.
- If you don't have a credit card, get one; if you can't qualify for one, get a secured credit card that reports to all credit bureaus. The credit line will usually equal the amount you have on deposit for security. Use the card regularly, and keep your balance low or pay in full; at a minimum, pay on time each month to avoid the steep interest rate. You can build a good payment and credit history this way; however, you should make sure that after about twelve months of paying the creditor in a timely manner, you qualify for their traditional card. Don't accept a crummy prepaid card, that is, one that charges an annual fee over sixty dollars or charges you an application fee.

- Until you can secure your own credit, piggyback on someone with good credit. As an authorized user, the credit history on the account will factor into your credit score, though it does not weigh as heavily as if it were your own. You can always have your name removed if the credit goes south. Simply call the creditor and ask to have your name removed, but understand that you may lose everything, including the history, depending on the creditor and credit bureau. There are no other risks for you because you are not responsible for the payment. The user will need to trust that you will not sabotage his or her credit, and you should be responsible.

- Obtain a mixture of credit when you are ready, for example, a mortgage, credit card, and a vehicle loan. This shows the lender you are responsible and capable of managing credit. A good mix of credit is also a factor in the payment history section of your report, worth 35 percent of your score.

- Pay down credit cards. Paying them down is more effective than paying down installment loans, such as a mortgage, car, or student loan. You should have a goal to keep credit card balances below 30 percent to maintain a good debt-to-credit ratio. Pay down cards closest to their limit and then the ones with the highest interest rate—or do it vice versa if your primary goal is to get out of debt and boosting your credit score is secondary.

- Dust off old credit cards, and use them strategically. Avoid having old established credit cards closed by the lender for nonuse, as this could mean losing your history and increasing your debt-to-credit ratio above 30 percent.

- Dispute any old debts that are incorrectly reported. Old and smaller debts are easier to dispute; usually small amounts are not investigated, just removed. Never pay a credit-repair service for something you can do yourself. If the debt is correct, a credit-repair company can't force the credit bureaus or lenders to remove accurately reported debt on your behalf.

- Dispute accounts that remain on your credit report once they are over seven and a half years old or ten years old for bankruptcies. After the above time frames have passed, the negative reporting on the debt should not remain on your report.

- Dispute late payments, charge-offs, reaged accounts, collections, or lower credit limits that are incorrect. Charge-offs in bankruptcy should not be on the credit report; sometimes when accounts are sold to new collectors, they try to reage the account in order to have more time to collect. Maintain old credit reports to prove the age of an account.

- Ask the creditor to remove late payments and reage the account if it's to your advantage. Let's say you are two months late on an account due to some personal reasons, and now you are able to pay. If they reage the account back to when you were paying timely, it is advantageous for you. However, after 180 days, creditors usually charge off your account from their books, and reaging may not be possible.

- Pay on time. Late payments hurt a good credit score more than they do a bad credit score; it can be as much as one hundred points against a good score and only seventy against a bad score.

- Be careful in how you open new credit. Although it only accounts for 10 percent of your score, it is still important. A lot of new credit all at once looks as if you are going to charge a load of merchandise, increasing your vulnerability to default. Use discretion when opening up new charges; don't open up an account just because they are offering 15 percent off today with a 21 percent interest rate later; you can hurt your credit and pay more interest. Opening new accounts will also lower the average account age. FICO score considers the age of your oldest account, the age of the newest account, and an average age of all your accounts. Opening new credit has an even larger effect on your score if you don't have a lot of other credit accounts.

CHAPTER 3

Getting out of Debt

Getting out of debt is a process, not an event, and far more gratifying than boosting your credit score; fortunately, getting out of debt often increases your credit score. Everyone should have at least one credit card. Credit cards can help improve our lives, enabling us to enjoy pleasures such as vacations, homes, cars, or even starting a business. If you have ever made a hotel or flight or even a car-rental reservation, you understand the importance of the credit card. What about purchasing concert tickets or making other purchases on the Internet? Same importance. You can use a debit card to purchase concert tickets, make hotel reservations, and so on, but your debit card is often tied to your bank account. With the advent of identity theft, a credit card can offer you protection that a debit card may not. The fact is credit cards are part of American culture, and you can't beat them for convenience. There are probably over a billion credit cards in circulation. The key is properly managing credit. Some use it positively and others irresponsibly. Improper or irresponsible actions can make us slaves to credit lenders.

Good debt is debt that provides future benefits and/or appreciates over time, such as a home mortgage or a college education. Bad debt is used for purchases that don't provide future value and/or depreciate quickly, for example, dining out or clothing purchases.

Generally debt is in one of two categories. Secured debt is secured by some collateral to reduce the risk for the lender. The lender has recourse if you don't pay your mortgage. Your house can be repossessed and resold to satisfy the debt. Unsecured debt is the opposite; these loans are not collateralized with a lien or asset. Unsecured loans are risky for the lender without the element of recourse; therefore, the interest rates are higher. An unsecured credit card is a perfect example.

Assuming you are able to make your payments on your debts, such as your home and car, and for services you need, such as utilities and so on, the following suggestions can help you get out of debt sooner.

- Make a list of your debts from the highest interest rate to the lowest.
- Create a budget. Don't let your wants exceed your budget; eliminate unnecessary expenses. You don't have to have all the latest gadgets or the most expensive car.

Debt-Reduction Strategy

- Find an extra $100 to $200. This could be from working a second job, eliminating unnecessary purchases such as designer coffee, using public transportation, doing your own hair, buying fewer gifts, or eating out a lot less. Use the extra money to pay off the lowest balance in the high-interest-rate category

- Once you have paid the balance in full, move on to the debt with the next-highest interest rate. In addition to the original payment of this debt, also use the extra $100 to $200 plus the payment you were previously making on the now paid-off balance. Continue in this pattern as shown in the example below.

January

DEBT	INTEREST RATE	BALANCE	PAYMENT	NEW PAYMENT
Credit card Nuvo	15%	$1,500	$75	$75
Installment AAA	12%	$3,000	$200	$200
Credit card Oleo	12%	$800	$50	$150 ($50 + extra $100)
Auto payment	8%	$17,000	$550	$550

July—Six months later, no additional purchases made (interest charges were considered)

DEBT	INTEREST RATE	BALANCE	PAYMENT	NEW PAYMENT
Credit card Nuvo	15%	$1,146	$75	$225 ($75+ $150)
Installment AAA	12%	$1,942	$200	$200
Credit card Oleo	12%	0	0	0
Auto payment	8%	$15,161	$550	$550

In this example, the credit card Oleo is paid off in six months, and the credit card Nuvo is paid off by the end of the year, with $225 monthly payments.

Continue this pattern until you are out of debt.

- Set up an emergency savings account. I know you are thinking, *I'm trying to get out of debt, so how can I put money aside?* It is crucial that you start and grow an emergency fund—even if you have to start with just twenty dollars a month. Not having an emergency fund probably put you in debt. For example, your car breaks down or needs major repairs. Do you have the money, or do you have to charge it? Or even worse, do you have to turn to the resources of a pawnshop or a payday loan for money, which usually means paying a lot in fees? To prepare for these situations, use a portion of your newfound money to start your emergency fund.
- Avoid using a credit card for unplanned expenses or impulse purchases.
- Sell some assets.
- Make a behavior change. If you are an impulse spender, stop.
- Don't fall for schemes such as prize guarantees, mortgage rescue schemes, work-at-home scams, or other credit-related scams. It's easy to fall prey to schemes offering to get you out of debt, especially if your finances are out of control. Be wary of any program that asks you for money up front or requires you to buy products or services as a condition or as a suggestion. Remember that if an offer is too good to be true, it probably is.

Avoiding Scams

A cousin on my mother's side was a victim of a magazine scam. Robert told everyone that he had won a $100,000 prize. Naturally, he was asked how he got so lucky. He explained that the magazine company had already declared him a winner, and all he had to do was buy a magazine subscription, a small price to pay in return for the cash prize. A month later, he was still optimistic, claiming that he had to buy another subscription, but he assured us that the money was on the way. This went on for several months. Eventually I guess he met the scam's purchase quota, because he told us that he had bought everything he needed to buy and was just waiting for the check in the mail. Well, he waited and waited until the realization hit him: he had been scammed. Robert was never the same after that. Embarrassed and out of hundreds of dollars, he eventually moved away a broken man. Robert was the perfect victim of mass advertising; surely someone vulnerable and in need of money would take a bite from the hook.

There are many credit card offers to help restore your credit if you are having difficulty obtaining credit elsewhere, but they come with steep costs. For example, one bank card offer requires a $95 initial processing fee, also known as a security deposit; a $75 annual fee the first year, the maximum allowed by the Credit CARD Act of 2009; a $45 annual fee in subsequent years; and a $6.25 monthly fee starting the second year. This is incentive enough to maintain good credit and never need this bank's assistance in restoring your credit. The first year, you will pay $170; the second and subsequent years you'll pay $120 in addition to the 49.9 percent interest rate on any outstanding balance you may carry on the low credit limit of about $300.

Pawnshop

I used the services of a pawnshop only once in my life. I was a teenager hanging out with my cousin visiting from out of town, and we wanted to buy pizza from the new Pizza Hut that had recently opened in our neighborhood. Our cash combined was hardly enough to buy the pizza pie we both craved. After racking our brains on how to raise cash, I noticed he was sporting a nice new watch on his arm; it looked expense, with a diamond on the 6 and the 12. I suggested that we pawn his watch now and gather the money later to retrieve it. He was reluctant but finally relented. I convinced him to pawn his watch just so we could split a large two-topping pizza. After our desires were satisfied, he had deep regrets, and so did I. We knew that when the broker handed us the pawn ticket and the $10.00, we had no means to raise the capital of $12.20 in thirty days. The amount sounds small, but that equates to 264 percent in yearly terms. The pawn ticket itemized the cost, 2 percent in interest and 20 percent in fees. Needless to say, he returned home without his watch, and it was a long time before he absolved me from my actions.

The experience taught me several lessons: don't borrow money that you have no means to repay, don't borrow money for items that don't add value, and, most importantly, people are more important than money.

Pawnshops have been around for thousands of years; they make collateral loans to people who have merchandise the broker is interested in buying. A pawnbroker specializes in loans and obviously has a good eye for market value on a variety of items. He or she must be able to resell the item if you don't return for it; selling your merchandise enables them to recoup their money plus a profit. Pawnshops give a small percentage of the items you leave with them for collateral in the form of a loan, which includes interest that varies from broker to broker. The interest is typically a lot more than traditional loan instruments, and don't forget the fees. The fees alone can be as much as 20 percent disguised under the charges for appraisal, storage, and insurance, which allows them to bypass regulated caps on interest-rate charges. To use a pawnshop, you'll only need proper identification, no credit or bank account. If you return for your merchandise and repay your obligation, the amount you were loaned plus a fee, you retrieve your merchandise. If you don't return, the pawnbroker keeps your collateral, which is what happened with my cousin's watch. The loan was paid in full when we walked out of the door with the cash in hand. If it's an item you really can't part with, you may exercise the option to renew for another thirty days with more interest and fees. Once your merchandise is left at the pawnshop, it usually becomes their inventory for sale, which makes a pawnshop a great place to shop.

Payday Loans

Let's say that your water heater is broken and you need a new one right away to take a warm bath. You are at your maximum debt-to-income limit, so you are unable to obtain financing at the retail store allowing you to pay over time. As a result you pay the $400 in cash for the water heater and installation cost. Paying for the water heater has left you short of paying your mortgage, which is already one month behind. You don't want to ask a friend or relative, because you have leaned on them too much in the past, so you turn to a payday loan for a short-term fix.

You visit an establishment where the shingle reads "Payday Loans Here." You only need to prove that you have income coming in, which you do. But they don't know or care that your current debts already exceed your income or that your credit score is low, so you write a check for the date of your next payday, two weeks away. When the due date arrives and you can't pay the entire amount because of your other obligations, you pay to renew the loan for a fee and roll over the original loan amount and original interest rate. This cycle continues until a lump sum of money comes your way, usually a tax refund check. By this time you will have paid unreasonable amounts, earning the lender huge profits.

Car-Title Loan

If you no longer have a lien on your vehicle—that is, you have paid the lien holder in full, usually a bank or finance company—you may be tempted to obtain a car-title loan when you can't make ends meet. It looks like a viable solution to your short-term problem, but it isn't. The terms are usually for thirty days, and the amount the lender will loan you depends on the value of the vehicle you put up for collateral and not based on your ability to repay the loan. Most lenders will loan you no more than 25 percent of the wholesale value of the vehicle; if you default on the loan, the lender wins. This type of predatory lending is costly to the borrower because interest rates can be as much as 300 percent.

The advertisement is enticing, dangling a 25 percent interest rate, one which you may think you can pay; after all some credit cards charge 25 percent or more. The 25 percent per month equates to 300 percent per year; this is relevant because most loans are extended past the thirty days, sometimes close to a year, because most borrowers lack the ability to pay unless they receive a lump-sum windfall. For every month the loan is extended, the lender charges a fee plus the current interest, which allows the borrower to roll it over again and again. At the end of the process, you will have paid more than twice the amount you borrowed, assuming you are able to pay off the loan. Oftentimes, the lender collects fees, interest, and your vehicle. Just to give you an idea of how bad these loans are, the 2006 Military Lending Act prohibits anyone from offering a car-title loan to active-duty service members and to their dependents. As of February 2013, twenty-one states are reported to engage in car-title lending.

You may be likely to fall prey to exorbitant predatory lending fees and interest if you meet this profile:

- earn less than $30,000
- are unmarried
- have less than a high school education
- rent your abode
- are unbanked
- have no savings

Internet Scams

Craig was laid off from his job as a customer service representative in 2009. He was vigilant in looking for new work, but the economy was unforgiving. An advertisement on the Internet caught his attention; they were looking for a mystery shopper. The pay sounded good, and he only had to do what he enjoyed doing, eating out at restaurants. Craig completed the online job application and immediately submitted it. He received an e-mail a few days later congratulating him on becoming a mystery shopper. Later, he received a certified cashier's check for $1,000 along with a letter; the letter instructed him to deposit the check into his bank account. He followed the instructions, including keeping all transactions a secret. Two days later, Craig was instructed to withdraw $900 in cash and take it to one of the restaurants he would later patronize. The remaining $100 stayed in his account as an advance payment. He met with whom he believed to be the owner, a professional in appearance. The "owner" accepted the cash and explained how and why he needed to transfer the money to the corporate office in Canada, which only took a few minutes. Just three days later, the bank sent Craig a letter explaining that the cashier's check he'd deposited was counterfeit, and he would need to pay back the $1,000 plus a $55 penalty.

Craig was an unwitting participant in an illegal scam, and the crooks had his Social Security number. He broke his silence and reported the scam to the police and confessed to a few of his friends.

CHAPTER 4

Saving and Investing Money

Saving

Once you are out of debt and/or your income exceeds your expenses, you can start to save. A good tip to remember along the way is if you receive a large lump sum of cash—perhaps from an inheritance, tax refund, insurance payment, or a bonus at work—don't spend it all; deposit some into savings or invest it. *USA Today* reported that a bank survey showed that 55 percent of women and 45 percent of men didn't have at least three months of emergency savings, which put them at risk of financially mishandling life's emergencies.

My cousin would struggle all year just to make ends meet. Every month she had to borrow a few extra dollars from a friend or relative to complete her mortgage payment or get gas and food in between paydays. This particular year, she received a federal tax refund for $4,360. I advised her to put some of the money away in savings and use some to pay off some debts so she would have both a rainy-day savings and less debt, enabling her to make ends meet at the end of the month. She didn't take my advice and spent the money within two months; the cycle of living paycheck to paycheck continued.

If she had saved the money in a non-interest-bearing account, dividing it into twelve months to use it each month for bills, she would have an extra $363 each month to cover expenses for a year, avoiding a payday loan or car-title loan.

On August 1, 2013, Congressman Serrano introduced the Financial Security Credit Act of 2013 to encourage household savings. In his bill, there is an incentive for low- to moderate-income households to save their tax refund. The congressman introduced several savings options, including options for the unbanked. If you maintain your refund deposit for up to eight months, you can qualify for a refundable credit of up to $500. Imagine the opportunity to build an emergency fund over just a few years. A similar program has proven to work in New York City; there is hope that this bill will pass and reach across the nation.

Why should you save money?

for capital on hand
for emergencies
for temporary unemployment
for investing

Capital on Hand

Let's say there is an opportunity to buy a house that the seller has just reduced to $75,000 below market value in the neighborhood you want to live in. The down payment you will need to buy this house is $5,000. If you are ready and prepared, you can take advantage of this opportunity.

Emergencies

If your car breaks down and you need $500 to fix it but don't have the money in your budget, what will you do? You could end up taking on credit card debt or a predatory loan if you don't have at least $500 saved.

Temporary Unemployment

You should always maintain a minimum of six months of monthly expenses in your savings; more is better. Without savings, you can be categorized as living paycheck to paycheck; missing one paycheck can leave you homeless or with bad credit. Your payment history is worth 35 percent of your FICO score.

First refer to your budget to determine how much discretionary income you have for saving. Set a goal of how much you want to save and why. You may have a goal of building an emergency fund, buying a home or a new car, or taking a vacation. Challenge yourself; set a time frame for when you want to accomplish your goal; track your progress, and find creative ways to increase your savings.

Talk to your company's payroll staff or your bank about allocating a set sum of money into a savings account through direct deposit. Don't allocate more than you can afford; if you do, you may accumulate debt for basic expenses.

Keeping your debt in check affords you the ability to save more. As debt dissolves, more money is available for saving. It is a good idea to pay off high-interest credit card debt from savings and allocate the payment you would have made to your savings.

Investing

Investing can afford you capital appreciation above the inflation rate, increasing your buying power, and help you build wealth. However, the first investment, and most important one, is to invest in your ability to pay your obligations and accumulate liquid emergency funds before you allocate funds for investing.

Why should you invest?

- to meet future goals of major purchases such as a car or a home, education, and retirement
- to have your money working for you
- to beat inflation
- for capital appreciation

Investments can include stocks, bonds, real estate, gold, and precious metals. The lottery is not an investment. *Money Magazine*'s managing editor, Craig Matters, describes the lottery as a tax on the mathematically challenged. Unfortunately, people who make less invest a higher percentage of their income in lotto tickets.

A savings account is also not an investment; the interest is usually less than the average inflation rate of 3 percent; however, it is a secure way to hold on to current funds that can be used later for investing. After a period of time, funds in savings accounts depreciate in value and have less purchasing power. If you deposited $1,000 in a savings account earning 2 percent interest annually, with a 3 percent inflation rate for the United States, in two years it will have buying power of only $980. Ideally, investments should appreciate in value.

It will take you thirty-five years to double any amount of money at an interest rate of just 2 percent but only nine years at a rate of 8 percent, which is possible with a good investment. The higher the interest rate, the faster your money will grow. If you don't have a financial calculator, you can use the rule of 72 to determine how long it will take to double your money; 72 is the dividend, and the interest rate is the divisor, for example, 72/2 or 72/8. The rule of 72 is fairly accurate and can provide you with a quick ballpark figure. A financial calculator will provide accurate calculations consistently.

Financial Calculator (PV=present value, I=interest rate, N=number of years, FV=future value)

PV = 1,000	PV = 1,000
I = 2	I = 8
N = 35	N = 9
FV = 2000	FV = 2000

Investing in stocks can return as much as 20 percent, and bonds can return as much as 6 percent. Regular savings accounts may not exceed a return of more than 2 percent; after accounting for inflation, it can be less than that.

With those kinds of results, you may ask yourself, why doesn't everyone invest?

- Risk—Stocks and bonds carry risk; you can lose the entire amount invested. If you want to be safe, your money is insured from loss up to $250,000 per account at the bank.
- Disposable income—Can you afford to invest? You must first refer to your budget. Your budget shows your routine expenses. You have disposable income to invest after you have paid routine expenses, saved for emergencies, and paid down your debt.

You can accumulate additional money for investing by stockpiling away money from these areas:

- gifts that you receive for Christmas, birthdays, and so forth
- a portion of weekly or monthly allowances
- skipping the four-dollar cup of coffee each day

Coffee price—$4.00 x 365 days

1 yr.	5 yrs.	10 yrs.
$1,460	$7,300	$14,600

Exercise

If you deposited $1,460 at the end of each year into a savings account earning 2 percent, how much would you have in five years? Thirty years? ($7,598, $59,229) If you invested the same amount in the stock market with an average rate of return of 10 percent, how much would you have in five years? Thirty years? ($8,913, $240,162) Time and interest add value to money; a high interest rate over a long period of time can yield a hefty sum.

Many invest to increase personal freedom, achieve a sense of security, and be able to afford the things they want in life. There are many investment vehicles. Which one is right for me? The right investment for you is based upon a number of factors: the amount of time before you need the money, your goals, and whether or not you are risk averse.

Stocks and Bonds

In most instances, the greater the risk, the greater the potential of a higher return on your money; you also risk a greater loss. You can reduce risk and protect your investments by diversifying your portfolio. Your investments shouldn't be perfectly correlated; this implies that as one security moves either up or down, the other security will move in the same direction. If you experience a catastrophic loss, all your investments will follow suit. You want investment A to gain more than enough to cover any losses from investment B, which is why you should never put all your eggs in one basket of investments. You want a perfectly negative correlation that will move in an equal amount in the opposite direction. It is rare that you will find a perfect negative correlation, but you can come close and manage your risk.

You may be a conservative investor, who doesn't want the risk of losing any money, or a moderate investor, who is willing to invest in some low- and some high-risk investments. You may be an aggressive investor, investing in a variety of high-risk investments.

Whatever your risk tolerance, everyone should invest in stocks and bonds during some part of their lives, if for nothing more than to share in the growth of this country and even in the world. You will first need to know some investing basics and how the stock market works.

Stock Market

The stock market is an arena where many people can invest money and possibly do well over long periods of time. The stock market is a place to buy a share of a particular company in the form of a stock. History has documented since the end of World War II an average return of about 10 percent, which is more than most other investments and enough to outpace inflation. But throughout the years, there have been both bear and bull returns. For these reasons, the market is both loved and feared.

Bull Market vs. Bear Market

A bull market exists when the economy is doing well, with low unemployment, rising gross domestic product, and, most importantly, rising stock prices. Most investments do very well during these times, but nothing lasts forever, and during a bull market there is a risk that stocks may rise to a point where they become overvalued and unaffordable.

A bear market is the opposite of the bull market. It is defined as a sustainable 20 percent decline in the market. It is characterized by recession, higher unemployment, and declining stock prices. A market correction is when there is between a 10 percent and 20 percent decline in the market.

How does a stock make it to the stock market?

When a company has a need to grow, to research, or to expand operations, there is usually a need for money. Either the money is borrowed, gained through the issuance of corporate bonds, or made from selling stock. When money is borrowed, it has to be repaid within the specified time and terms; in other words, there is a contractual agreement. When bonds are issued there is an obligated to timely repay bondholders principal and interest. If stock is sold, the company sells the shares to the public and offers the investors ownership in the company. Investors who purchase stock own a portion of the company, consequently becoming shareholders, however small or large the percentage may be. The company has given up equity and now answers to the shareholders.

Where can you buy stocks in the United States?

Direct Purchase

You can buy stock directly from a publicly traded company if they offer a direct stock purchase plan (DSPP). Check the website of the company you are interested in. You can also call or e-mail its investor-relations department. Usually they offer the option of a onetime minimum investment or enrollment in their automatic investment plan, where money is automatically withdrawn from your account at regular intervals for purchases. If your monthly allotment doesn't cover the cost of a single share, you can purchase fractions of a share. Most companies offer automatic dividend reinvestment if they pay dividends. Monthly interval payments allow you to take advantage of dollar-cost averaging: when stock prices are low, you can afford more; when prices are higher, you purchase less to avoid the risk of paying a large sum for a single investment at the wrong time.

The big advantage of buying directly from a single company is usually there is no commission charge. The disadvantage is the lack of diversification; you are only buying one particular stock. Alternatively, for a fee, you can utilize services that will allow you to invest in several companies. Also, with this method the trades are usually not in real time; the stock price could be higher or lower when your trade is actually executed.

Stockbrokers

A full-service broker can be costly; however, you benefit from his or her investment research and advice. Discount brokers such as E*TRADE, T-D Ameritrade, and Scottrade usually have lower trading costs. It's easy to establish an account online with them and use their resources to conduct your own research and benefit from their analyst-written advice. The cost of trades can depend on your online account balance. The higher the balance, the lower the cost. In either case the cost will be less than a full-service broker and more than a deep-discount broker, who typically does not offer as much in resources.

Brokers trade stocks, bonds, and other securities on stock exchanges, the most important component of the stock market. Most large US stocks are traded on the New York Stock Exchange (NYSE) and the National Association of Securities Dealers Automated Quotations (NASDAQ).

US Stock Exchanges

NYSE. The New York Stock Exchange is probably the world's largest exchange based on market value, representing one-third of trades worldwide. It was established in 1817 and has listed as many as 2,308 stocks. Some specialists actually execute trades on the floor of the NYSE, located at 11 Wall Street, Lower Manhattan, New York City, New York. They also trade equities electronically.

NASDAQ. Technology stocks are mostly traded on this exchange. Although headquartered in New York, it also allows the execution of trades electronically, which is usually faster and less expensive.

You will likely find small-capitalized stocks and start-ups on the Alternext, CAC Small, SDAX, and TecDAX exchanges. There are also other trading venues, including the over-the-counter market.

There are specific requirements for inclusion in a specific exchange, such as minimum number of shares outstanding, minimum market capitalization, and minimum annual income. Various stock exchanges are located throughout the world, for example, the London Stock Exchange and the Tokyo Stock Exchange.

Stock Indexes

You have no doubt heard news reports on the status of the market based on indexes. For example, the Dow Jones Industrial Average (DJIA) is up 16 points to 16,500 today, or the S&P index gained 2.51 points or 0.1 percent to 2,101, or NASDAQ Composite moved toward the 5,000 mark 15.67 points to 4,982.

These indexes move up and down based on consumer confidence, that is, their expectations of certain companies' earnings and risk. Different indexes measure different segments of the market. Segments could include large-cap, small-cap, international, technology, and so on. Stock indexes have specific requirements to become a member of a particular index.

Dow Jones Industrial Average (DJIA). The DJIA was founded in 1882 by Charles Dow, Edward Jones, and Charles Bergstresser. It is the most popular index and represents one-fourth of the value of the entire market and measures the movement of thirty large, influential US stocks. The Dow is price weighted, calculated by adding the prices of the thirty stocks and dividing them by the Dow divisor, which is modified when necessary. Previously the share prices of the thirty stocks were added and divided by thirty, which didn't accurately account for various corporate actions. The Dow measures the large-cap segment of the market; stocks in this index are selected by a committee based on certain qualifiers. Only General Electric has the prestigious honor of having remained on the DJIA since its inception.

The DJIA index can be down sixteen points, but your stock can be up even if it is listed within the index. Some stocks move in the opposite direction of the market; in addition, your stock may not be in the segment that the index is representing. To determine the tendency of your stock movement in relation to the market, look at the stock's beta. The beta establishes a relationship between your stock and the rest of the market. If your stock has a beta of one, it means your stock will have a tendency to move with the market. A beta of more than one can be more volatile than the market, but rewards can be higher. Stocks with a beta of less than one are less volatile than the market. You can buy exchange-traded funds (ETF) that follow the same strategy of an index. For example, you can buy an ETF that tracks the Dow or the S&P 500; when the index goes up or suffers catastrophic losses, your portfolio will move in tandem.

Standard & Poor's (S&P 500). This index tracks five hundred of the most popularly traded stocks from a diverse segment of the market, selected by an S&P index committee. It has become the leading index, tracking the movement of large market-capitalization stocks and is a benchmark for the overall market. The S&P contains over 70 percent of the US stock market value, which is why it provides a better indication of total market movement in the marketplace.

NASDAQ Composite Index. Not to be confused with the NASDAQ exchange, the NASDAQ Composite Index tracks all the stock that is listed on the NASDAQ exchange. It is market-capitalization weighted and includes both US and international stocks; it is heavily weighted with technology stock, which represents the major movements, but includes other market segments. The NASDAQ includes large-cap, small-cap, and speculative stocks that may not be well established.

Wilshire 5000. This index tracks more than five thousand stocks, closer to seven thousand US stocks, making it one of the broadest indexes. It's not as popular as the S&P 500 although more comprehensive. This market-rated index includes companies with a wide range of market values from every industry. Higher-value stocks tend to overweight the index, and lower-value stock underweight the index. It's designed to give the big picture of the overall market.

Russell 2000. This index is market-capitalization weighted and tracks the movement of a diverse segment of small-capitalization stocks in the market.

What incentive would an investor have to purchase shares of stock in a company? An investor may expect the company to perform well and perhaps outperform others in the same sector. If you own a share of a company whose product is in high demand, you can expect higher earnings. If earnings of a company rise, the company may share earnings with the shareholders in the form of cash dividends. An investor can reinvest the dividends received to purchase more stock through a dividend-reinvestment plan at little or no cost or they can elect to receive the dividend payment. Companies don't always pay dividends; they may choose to retain some or all of the earnings for future growth or for other reasons.

Some companies never pay dividends. Therefore the expected appreciation of the stock price is what the investor relies upon for a return on his or her investment. Capital gains occur when you sell the stock for more than your basis in the stock minus sales commission. Your base consists of the purchase price and purchase commission. Commissions can range from ten to fifty dollars per transaction, which is why most investors buy large blocks of stock, minimizing the cost associated with several small transactions for the same stock.

Your total return from a stock is an accumulation of dividends and capital gains. Dividends are generally taxable in the year received; capital gains are taxable in the year of the sale, unless the sale or dividend payments are part of a retirement account or some other deferred account. The dividends are reported on line 8 of the federal tax form 1040, and the capital gain is reported on the supporting schedule D. More on taxes later.

What determines the price of a stock?

Economic growth plays an important role in the price of stock. When the demand for product rises, the company produces more goods and services, thereby increasing the company's income. Take, for example, the company Apple. On April 23, 2014, *USA Today* reported that Apple announced quarterly sales of $46.6 billion and net profit of $10.2 billion, beating analysts' projections of $43.5 billion in revenue. Apple reported strong iPhone and iPad sales and record revenue from services during the quarter. After the news, the stock price increased over 8 percent. More goods and services create more jobs and higher income. With more money, consumers buy more products, driving the demand higher, resulting in higher sales for the company and higher stock prices. When the economy is weak, the demand for products is low; companies may have to lay off workers. Less money is available, so a lower demand for products produces lower sales. Consequently, the price of the stock declines. Governments' fiscal policies also play a role in consumer spending habits.

When determining what strategies to use for investing, you should first invest for the long term, although day traders make tons of money speculating and seizing opportunities on short-term movement of stock prices. Some may consider this a form of gambling. A good investment strategy also includes a portfolio with high-quality stocks, bonds, no-load mutual funds, and exchange-traded funds.

Analyzing Stocks

First, let's start by interpreting basic information about a stock. The most up-to-date stock quotes can be obtained online. Other sources include the media and financial papers such as the *Wall Street Journal*.

Verizon Wireless (VZ)

Open	48.73	Market Cap	201.98B
52-Week High	53.66	Shares Outstanding	4.1B
52-Week Low	45.08	Dividend Payable	8/1/2014
Volume	16,467,568	Next Earnings Date	10/21/2014
P/E	10.35	Yield	4.35%
Beta	0.4	Quarterly Dividend	.53
EPS	4.705	Next Dividend Date	7/18/2014

Source E*Trade

Dividends represent the amount paid, if any; it can be expressed quarterly or annually. Verizon pays a .53 quarterly / $2.12 yearly dividend,

Yield is the annual dividend expressed as a percentage of the stock price: it's a return on your investment for a stock. It determines how much cash flow you will receive for each dollar invested. A high-dividend yield can provide a stable cash flow. Verizon's dividend yield is 4.35 percent ($2.12/48.73). An investment in one hundred shares of Verizon stock would cost you $4,873; you could expect a yearly dividend payment of $212.

Market cap is total value of the shares of stock issued. The outstanding shares are multiplied by the stock price.

EPS represents the net income of the company expressed per share, in this case $4.70. When calculated, the net income is divided by the weighted average of outstanding common stock shares (preferred stock dividends are subtracted from net income before the calculation). Verizon is sharing $2.12 of earnings with common-stock shareholders. The higher the earnings, the more the company has to share.

P/E is a ratio of a stock's price to its current or forecasted annual earnings per share. Sometimes companies use the last four quarters of EPS, known as the trailing P/E, or the next four quarters, known as the leading or projected P/E, or a combination of both. A negative EPS means that the company is not profitable and is probably not a good investment. The average P/E is between fifteen and twenty, based on market conditions and the particular industry. Stable companies tend to have a lower P/E than growth companies. The P/E is referred to as the multiple of the stock; it tells how much an investor is willing to pay for each dollar of earning.

Verizon's P/E is calculated below. Investors are willing to pay $10.35 for every dollar earned per share.

$$\text{Share Price/EPS} = 48.73/4.705 = 10.35$$

Beta represents how close an investment tracks its benchmark and describes its volatility. A beta of one suggests that the stock moves with its benchmark.

Stock prices can rise depending on the current and future projected performance of the company. Performance is tied to demands for the product or service and corresponding sales. When investors heard the news that AT&T would be buying DirecTV for $50 billion and would be retaining management as a unit of AT&T, DirecTV stock increased by nearly $2 during trading hours; after-hours trading increased the price another $5.

Companies that are publicly traded create an annual report that contains financial information. The report includes a letter from the chief executive officer (CEO) summarizing recent performance and expected performance.

Investors can analyze the stock's financials for strengths and weaknesses and draw a conclusion based on investment goals. The annual report also includes the balance sheet and income statement, which is what you can use to help select a stock. Be sure to analyze the company quantitative and qualitative indicators.

You should understand the business model of the company you are interested in—understand how the company makes its money. Take, for example, Dell, which became an innovator with laptops. Instead of holding an inventory of computers that quickly become outdated, Dell operated by using a just-in-time business model, essentially eliminating stale inventory and eliminating the middleman by selling directly to the consumer. With a brilliant concept and outstanding customer service coupled with an affordable product, Dell was able to increase market shares, and it was a good buy.

You should determine if the company is able to maintain a competitive edge or if the market is easy to enter. Although Dell's name was highly recognized in personal-computer sales, its stock plummeted in the advent of computer price wars. Profit margins waned with the decline in demand for personal computers, which were being replaced by tablets and smartphones.

Does the company have good management? Of course you can read their bio on the company's website, but that information will not reveal any missteps or other negative information about them. You can compare their past performances to draw conclusions. For example, does the company follow the rules, or is it often sued?

Who are the customers of the company? Are they a small or a large segment of the market? These are questions that should be answered. Will the company grow, or is the market already saturated, making it necessary to woo customers from competitors?

Some valuations are based on historical price patterns—for example, purchasing stock that has risen for three consecutive days, expecting the trend to continue. Conversely, if the stock has continually declined for several days, you may want to sell or decide not to buy. The historical price pattern is not a foolproof method, and there are so many other factors to be considered.

Other methods consider the financial ratios to determine if the stock is a sound investment and if you are receiving a value. Valuing stock is based on the value of the company's earnings. This method is based on the concept of the higher the earnings, the more money the company has to pay dividends to shareholders or to reinvest for further expansion, which will generate more earnings.

The P/E is the most popular way to compare the relative value of stocks based on earnings, calculated by taking the current price of the stock and dividing it by the EPS. This tells you whether a stock's price is high or low relative to earnings. P/E is often used to determine if a stock is a good buy. Investors may see a low P/E as a bargain and a high P/E as expensive, but it's complex; other factors are involved, such as interest rates, expected earnings, and dividend payments.

If all the analyzing and researching is not your cup of tea, you can let fund managers, for a fee, do the work for you by investing in quality no-load mutual funds and exchange-traded funds.

Investing is not just about stocks and bonds; it can also include investing in real estate or starting your own business. There are a host of other investment instruments; we will discuss some of the others.

Money Market Accounts

Money market accounts earn slightly higher than a savings account. The higher rate comes with some restrictions; the number of withdrawals may be limited, and depending upon the type of money market account, it may or may not be FDIC insured. The minimum deposit may be a little higher; some require a $1,000 minimum initial deposit. When the stock market is volatile, or if you are risk averse, a money market account is a good, safe investment. Often assets are invested in low-risk T-bills, CDs, and commercial paper.

Certificates of Deposit (CDs)

CDs generally are insured by the FDIC and pay a slightly higher interest rate than a savings account with no risk up to the FDIC-insured amount. A CD is not very liquid; you can't make withdrawals from it until it matures, unless you pay a hefty penalty. Maturity rates can be from as little as three months to up to ten years. The longer the period, the higher the rate—but the difference is not substantial enough to outweigh the interest-rate risk. For example, if you open a five-year CD at an interest rate of 1.5 percent because the one-year and two-year CDs were paying 1.0 and 1.2 percent, respectively, and after two years the economy turns around and interest rates rise to 5 percent or 6 percent, you can't take advantage without withdrawing the money and incurring a penalty.

I Bonds

I Bonds keep pace with inflation, are issued by the federal government, and can be cashed after six months; otherwise, they continue to earn interest above the inflation rate.

CHAPTER 5

Purchasing a Vehicle

One of the biggest items on your budget, other than rent or mortgage, is probably the purchase of a vehicle. Most people are guided by their wants and not their budgets or future goals. A car has come to represent a certain status, causing a luxury-car craze. Henry Ford, the great automaker, built the Model T in 1908, a car that most people could afford comfortably. He was able to underprice his competitors for similar vehicles. When luxury vehicles hit the market, consumers had to have the newest and the latest. Henry Ford, a brilliant entrepreneur and billionaire, was appalled and didn't think that consumers should squander their money on luxury cars. I happen to agree with him; think of your budget and future goals.

Expensive car payments can remain on your budget for five years or more as opposed to two years for a used car or three to four years for a new, reasonably priced car.

Before you make that giant leap, decide what type of vehicle you need. A two-door coupe may not be sensible for someone who transports two to three children regularly. You might consider a car that delivers more than thirty miles per gallon if your daily commute is lengthy. Most car consumers want to invest in safe vehicles; visit www.safercar.gov for federal crash results to see how your car ranks.

You have the option of leasing or buying; in any event, they both may come with a high-pressure salesperson who will try to persuade you to buy what you can't afford or charge you more than the car is worth. Yes, you can negotiate the cost of a leased vehicle, and you should.

First, determine how much you can afford—consider the down payment, monthly payment, depreciation, interest on financing, taxes, fees, insurance premiums, fuel, maintenance, repairs, and gas. You can visit Edmunds. com in the "True Cost to Own" section to get an idea of the yearly cost to own your vehicle. Edmunds has a great comparison between similar cars with different costs to own. They compare two midsize family sedans— the purchase price of one is $21,500, and the other, $22,400. As a natural instinct, you might decide to buy the cheaper one, saving almost $1,000. But in the grand scheme of things, you end up paying more over a five-year ownership period. In the Edmunds example, the cheaper car to buy was actually more expensive to own. Over five years, it cost $33,438 to drive the car with the lower initial price. The more expensive car only cost $30,140 to drive over five years.

Cost to Own

- oil changes
- gasoline
- repairs/maintenance

- auto insurance
- taxes

Automobile Insurance

Automobile insurance can be expensive on a new vehicle; consider the initial risk the insurance companies have. Imagine that you drive your new car off the lot and immediately are involved in an accident that is, unfortunately, your fault. You are responsible for your damaged vehicle and the one you damaged. Your $28,000 new car is totaled and no longer useful. Immediately, you file a claim with the insurance company because the damages far exceed your deductible. The insurance company is responsible for the replacement of your car and the repairs of the other vehicle; meanwhile, you haven't made your first insurance premium payment.

You should speak with your insurance agent or potential agent to get a quote on the car that you are interested in before you make the purchase; you may be able to afford the car but not the insurance. It's usually cheaper to replace a used nonluxury vehicle; consequently, the premium is cheaper. Ask your insurance agent what you can do to decrease your premiums. For example, taking a defensive-driving course online could lower your premium considerably, or you may have the option to manage your bill online, another considerable savings. You can even capitalize on discounts for paying your premium in full. These are just a few; develop a relationship with your agent, and find out what other discounts you may qualify for. Sometimes the make, model, or color of the car makes a big difference in premium.

Researching Your Vehicle

You will need to do some homework—research and comparison shop—before you make your final decision on which car to purchase. Below are some good places to begin your search.

Consumer Reports. This publication provides unbiased ratings and recommendations for a host of products and services. You can read it at your library for free or purchase it at a bookstore or get a subscription at www.consumerreports.org.

MyProductAdvisor.com. On this website, you can select the features that are important to you in a car and then see several recommendations based on those features.

Edmunds.com. This website's "Total Cash Price" section lists the total typical expenses related to the purchase of the vehicle. The "True Cost to Own" section gives an estimated cost to own the vehicle over a five-year period. Edmunds also provides a good idea about how fast your car will depreciate, which can be useful if you plan to resell the vehicle or lease it.

After you have narrowed your search down to the car that is right for you, determined the cost to own the vehicle, and figured out whether you can afford the car, it's time to get the best deal on the vehicle of your choice. Below is a list of a few sites that can help you get a good deal.

FightingChance.com. This site helps you conduct a competitive bidding process from your home.

Autobytel.com. On this site, you can receive a free no-hassle, low-price quote, including a list of car prices and dealer costs.

Edmunds.com. You can also research and compare car prices on this site and view manufacturer incentives and rebates.

You should never pay the sticker price on the car. If you do, it probably means you need to brush up on your research and negotiation skills. Our instinct is to begin negotiating down from the sticker price, when in fact we should always negotiate up from the dealer cost, allowing room for dealer profit. Experts say, a good time to negotiate the price on a car is in November and December because not many people are interested in purchasing cars during the holiday season; it's just not a priority. This is the time for family and friends, cooking, and trimming the tree. This could mean manufacturer incentives and deals from the dealer for you. Not to mention that they want to end the year with a bang and some take-home bucks for the holidays too. Sales tend to decline during cold weather, thus creating an opportunity for you to venture out on a bitterly cold day for a good deal.

Late summer is also a good time to buy a car, with the arrival of new models and dealers scrambling to clear out last year's models. If these months are not good for you, try for the end of any month, when salespeople are trying to meet sales quotas. In any case, you should not be in a need-to-buy situation. In fact, you should never buy the same day. Salespeople have a way of wearing you down, and you usually end up making a bad deal; using the walkout method sometimes gets you the best deal.

As mentioned earlier, knowledge of the dealer's cost and markup is the best advantage you can have in negotiating. But now the dealers know that you know, because the Internet has made car buying more transparent. The Internet has effectively evened the playing field for those who research before a purchase. However, evidence has shown that the dealer cost is no longer fully disclosed on the invoice sheet or online. Some vehicle search sites provide market or target prices of what others have paid for similar cars; rarely does this price represent the dealer's cost. For a fee, *Consumer Reports* provides a pricing report that gives you the bottom-line price to use in negotiating. On Edmunds.com or Kelly Blue Book, KBB.com, you can find the invoice price that is supposed to represent what the dealer paid for the car; however, there may be dealer incentives and rebates you are not aware of. Manufacturer-to-dealer incentives lower the dealer's cost; make sure you find out about those at Edmunds.com and KBB.com. Knowing the incentives the dealer receives will give you more negotiating power to lower your bid. Once you have this information, you should end your bid somewhere around 2 percent above the invoice price, allowing the salesperson a reasonable commission.

After you complete your research and homework, you will most likely pay less for the vehicle than the customer who did not research or negotiate the price, because the car industry can't bolster its profits if everyone gets a good deal.

Sales Contract

Never sign a contract before reading it, and negotiate terms you don't agree with. Make sure there are no blank spaces. Blank spaces provide an opportunity for unscrupulous behavior; the dealer or the dealer's representative can add items to the contract that you didn't agree to, for example, expensive insurance that you will never use because you are not aware of its existence.

Buying a car is expensive, which is why most people obtain a loan for its purchase. It's a good idea to secure your financing in advance; a good place to start is with your banking institution or credit union. First, decide how much you can afford based on your budget, and then request the amount on your loan application. The bank or credit union will determine if you are credit worthy and what interest rate you qualify for based on your FICO score. If you obtain your financing at the dealer, you may be subjected to creative financing. If the salesperson asks you how much you can afford to pay, it's the introduction to creative financing. You could end up paying what you can afford to pay for a long period of time and a lot more, when you factor in the high interest rate.

Exercise: Based on your budget and savings, how much can you afford to put down, and how much can you afford each month?

Using a financial calculator, determine the monthly payment for a $20,000 vehicle with $1,000 down from savings for forty-eight months with a credit score of 740, and interest rate of 7.5 percent. ($459.40)

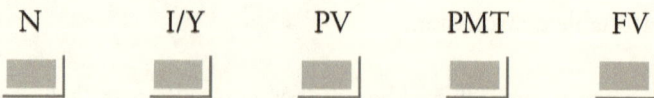

N	I/Y	PV	PMT	FV

Paying too much for a car can make a difference for the average family on a budget and delay meeting your goals. You can have the slick new car now that destroys your budget, or you can be practical and savvy. Consider purchasing a used car that fits your budget better.

Used-Car Purchase

Purchasing a used car can be intimidating in your quest for the best deal. Consider purchasing a certified used car from a dealer, which may provide you protection from buying a lemon. In addition, you are more likely to receive a clear title from a reputable dealer. Purchasing from an individual can be a bit risky; you can end up with no title or a salvage title. A salvage title could mean that the car has been deemed unsalvageable by the insurance company, or the car may have been rebuilt and possibly is unsafe to drive. On the other hand, you could get a better deal if you take the right steps. With cash on hand, you can avoid monthly payments or have very low payments if you are unable to pay in full. Used-car loans usually carry a higher interest rate than a newer car purchase, and the terms are usually shorter. The risk for the lender is higher because the car is older; it could have a major breakdown, and you may walk away from the loan without funds to repair it and make the payments too.

I agreed to go with a friend to buy a used vehicle at a used-car dealer. My friend had sketchy credit but had heard that this dealer worked well with customers with low credit scores. I noticed that all the vehicles on the lot were between ten to twelve years old but carrying price tags of new vehicles. The car my friend was interested in cost $20,000; it was twelve years old and was the cheapest on the lot. The salesman offered the following terms: five years at $400 a month based on my friend's paycheck stub. My friend was desperate for a car; he needed reliable transportation for work, and his poor credit made him an easy target for a bad deal. The salesman ran his credit and determined that he needed a cosigner, so all eyes were on me. I explained to him and the salesman that I was not willing to become responsible for payments my friend couldn't make. Although the cars were cosmetically maintained, there was a risk that a twelve-year-old car, probably worth $5,000, would require major repairs within the five-year period. In addition, it would be difficult if not impossible to resell a seventeen-year-old car.

You have probably heard of the three-day cooling-off period used in business—the one that allows you, the purchaser, and the seller a period after entering into a new contract to relieve yourselves from any obligation without penalty. You have until midnight the third business day after the contract date to cancel a deal you have entered into. Saturday is considered a business day—Sundays and holidays are not. One caveat, the cancellation must be in writing; however, no reason is necessary other than you changed your mind. Have you ever purchased something and wished you hadn't, realized you couldn't afford that impulsive buy, or been pressured by a pushy salesperson? For those reasons, this law was written. Different types of transactions will have different cooling-off rules, and not all types of contracts have such a provision; you should inquire before you sign your name to the contract. In fact, there is no three-day right to cancel on a new or used car, choose wisely.

Some used cars are sold as is, and some with a warranty. Keep the buyer's guide that the dealer is required to give you with the sale. It determines if there is a warranty. Even if it is sold as is, the buyer's guide may say differently. The dealer may make you promises and guarantees about what they will do after the sale in an effort to sell you a vehicle. For example, the dealer may say he will guarantee repairs for six months or say you can return the vehicle after thirty days. Get any guarantees from the dealer in writing, and read everything before signing.

Don't forget you are covered by a very important warranty that happens to be implied; it's not written or verbally spoken. It is a warranty of merchantability, that is, a product should perform to its implied standard. In this case, a car should do what it is designed to do—run. This warranty does not cover things that could go wrong, including a breakdown or the condition of the car. Private sales are not covered by implied warranties or state law.

Continue to follow the same criteria you would for a new car in meeting your needs when looking for a used car. Look for individual sellers who are perhaps selling an old car to upgrade to a new or bigger car or someone selling his or her assets just before moving or for reasons other than trying to unload a lemon onto an unsuspecting buyer.

Take your time and conduct a test-drive on the car you are interested in; a wise decision is to have a trusted mechanic of your choice do a thorough inspection. Ask for the maintenance records.

Try these sites to determine the value of the used car before you negotiate the price:

KellyBlueBook.com. Use this site to determine what your used car is worth.

NADA.com. Use this site to determine the value of the car.

Edmunds.com. Use this site to determine if the car is a good buy. You can get an appraised value, car reviews, and customer reviews. For example, a review of the Nissan Altima sedan 2.5L four-cylinder shows that the average price for a 2012 model is $15,354. It has responsive steering and a quiet ride, but the backseat is small compared to its rivals.

National Insurance Crime Bureau (NICB). Use this site to check the history of a car using its VIN number.

Exercise: Find the true cost to own a vehicle over a five-year period. Will the monthly payments and maintenance costs fit into your budget? Do you see the big picture and not just the price tag?

Leasing a Car

Why lease a vehicle? You have many of the same responsibilities of owning a vehicle, including maintenance, certain repairs, gas, and insurance. Leasing may be the right choice for some, especially if you want to drive a new car every two to four years. It can be pricey if you don't know the rules or if it's not the right decision for your situation. Conceptually, you expect to pay considerably less in monthly lease payments than a loan payment, but most leases have huge upfront costs and mileage restrictions. In addition, most vehicle lease owners pay too much. But how do you know if you're paying too much if you don't understand how the lease works? When you lease a vehicle, you pay for the depreciation of the negotiated car value. You need to be savvy to get a good deal, and you should be aggressive. The price you pay includes upfront costs such as the acquisition fee, security deposit, and processing fee; ask the dealer to waive upfront costs. Nearly every lease can be negotiated. In order to be an effective negotiator, you must be armed with information. Get more information about the car from places such as Edmunds.com, just as you would on a purchase.

Your lease payment is composed of the following three components:

1. Depreciation fee
2. Finance fee
3. Sales taxes

Let's start by understanding the lingo, which will lead to understanding how the lease is calculated.

Net capitalized cost. Negotiated sale price + dealer fees – trade-in value – down payment – rebates

Residual value. This is the predicted resale value of the car at the end of the lease. The residual percentage is provided by the dealer. For example, if the residual value is 60 percent, you would multiply .60 times the manufacturer's suggested retail price—the sticker price, not the negotiated price. Most cars have a residual value between 45 and 60 percent for a three-year lease.

It's not a good idea to enter into a lease for more than three years, as the bumper-to-bumper warranty is usually in place for three years and after that you may incur major expense that you are responsible for.

Depreciation. Some things appreciate with time, such as a home or a good wine vintage, but not an automobile; it depreciates. In fact it depreciates rapidly, especially during the first five years. The Internal Revenue Service assigns a five-year useful life to automobiles used for business, allowing you depreciation deductions for those five years. In a leasing deal, you pay the leasing company for depreciation over the terms of the lease, accounting for the loss in value.

sticker price of car	$25,000
negotiated price	$22,500
down payment	($1,000)
rebate	($500)
dealer fees	$1000
net cap. cost	$22,000
term	3 years
residual value	$12,500 [$25,000 x .50]

Depreciation fee. [(22,000 – 12,500) / 36] = $263.88

The depreciation you pay for the lease is calculated in the following manner: (net cap. cost – residual) / term of the lease. The lower the net cap. cost, which relies heavily on your negotiation skills, the lower your monthly payment. A low net cap. cost is advantageous because the residual percentage is based on the sticker price.

The base amount for the lease is $263.88; now we will need to add to that number the financing fees

Finance fee. (net cap. cost + residual) x money factor

You will pay interest on both the net cap. cost and residual value, because the dealer does not have the opportunity to sell the car until you return it and the dealer's funds remain tied up in the purchase of the vehicle.

When you review your lease, you will probably see your net cap. cost and the residual value but not the money factor, so you may not know what the finance fee consists of. Your credit score plays a vital role in this rate. Sometimes dealers only reveal this number as your lease charge or rental charge over the entire lease, for example, $3,000. Ask the dealer for your interest rate, or the money factor used in the calculation. It's easy to convert the money factor into your interest rate, simply multiply the money factor by 2400. It is a good idea to verify that your rate is comparable to new-car loan interest rates and it reflects your credit score. If your money factor is .0024, your annual interest rate is 5.76 percent.

Finance fee. $34,500 x .0024 = $82.80

So far, your monthly payment in this example is $345.68, the finance fee plus the depreciation fee. Unless you pay the taxes up front, the applicable sales tax would apply to the monthly lease payment.

Sales Tax. $345.68 x 7% = $24.27

Total lease payment = $369.95

You are paying the difference between the car's cost and the residual value of the car at the end of the lease. The residual value may be low, based on the car you choose; some cars hold their value while others don't. You want to lease a car that has a low depreciation rate. Your car can depreciate from 11 to 20 percent driving off the lot and between 15 and 25 percent the next four years. The range is so vastly different in the first year because it is based on how well you negotiated the deal. For example, if the car's MSRP is $25,000 and you paid $25,000, the dealer will buy back the car the same day at the wholesale price they paid, in this case $20,000. The car is now worth 20 percent less to the dealer. After the fifth year, depreciation begins to slow down, which is long after a lease ends. Leasing agents use the proffer of fifteen thousand miles driven each year to set the standard for depreciation.

If you had purchased the same car at the net cap. cost of $22,000 over a three-year period, with an interest rate of 5.76 percent, your monthly payment would be $666.89; over a four-year period, $514.15; and over a five-year period, $422.87.

Exercise

Think about some of the advantages and disadvantages of both buying and leasing.

CHAPTER 6

Buying a Home

Buying a home can provide you with a huge tax advantage, one you won't get from renting. Purchasing a home is also a major expense with a long-term commitment, unlike renting. Most people will need a mortgage loan to spread the payments over a period of time in order to afford a home. Purchasing a home is a good way to build wealth; the net worth of a homeowner is normally higher than that of a renter. Real estate normally appreciates on average of 3 to 5 percent per year. The value of your home minus the remaining mortgage balance equals your home equity, one of the largest sources of net worth. Homeowners are able to borrow against their equity to purchase other assets, such as a second home, or even to start a business.

If you look at the amortization schedule of a home loan, you will see that most homeowners pay more than double the original cost of the home when you factor in the interest payments, taxes, and insurance over a thirty-year period. It may look more like a consumption cost and not like a sound investment. It actually is a sound investment when you consider the fact that you have to pay to live somewhere, and this way you accomplish that and also build equity.

There are several types and terms of loans to choose from when buying a home. You should choose the one that is right for you and your budget without taking on risky loan terms or taking on a mortgage you can't afford.

Fixed-Rate Loans

Fixed-rate loans are most popular; because your interest rates are fixed, your payment will be stable, except for fluctuations in taxes and insurance. Fixed-rate-loan interest rates are slightly higher than some of the others we will talk about. We can use the loan information below to compare the different rates.

$165,000 loan	Interest rate—6%	Term—30, 20, 15	Extra payment—?

Thirty-year fixed rate. A thirty-year fixed-rate loan stretches your payment over a thirty-year period, making your payments more affordable. For a $165,000 loan with an interest rate of 6 percent, your principal and interest payment will be $989.26. You will pay more interest over the life of the thirty-year loan versus the twenty- or fifteen-year loan; in fact, you'll pay more in interest than in principal for the first eighteen years. Those interest payments in most cases are fully deductible on your tax return if you itemize deductions, which reduces your tax liability.

You can reduce the term of a thirty-year loan by six years without the benefit of a lower rate if at the beginning of the loan you make an extra $100 payment toward principal. You can reduce the term by ten years if you make an extra $200 payment toward principal each month.

How is that possible? Assuming you make all payments in a timely manner, the amortization on the loan changes. Amortization is the recalculation of the interest and principal each month. The interest rate is compounded twelve times a year, each month. As the principal goes down, however slightly or substantially, the rate is recalculated and applied to the outstanding balance; therefore, your payments are less toward interest and more toward principal.

Twenty-year fixed rate. This loan stretches your payments over a twenty-year period; your payment will be $1,182.11, which is higher than the thirty-year fixed-rate loan, but you will pay less in interest over the life of your loan, $118,706 versus $191,133 on a thirty-year loan. Principal exceeds interest in year nine, half the time it takes on a thirty-year loan. The interest payments are fully deductible in most cases as well.

Fifteen-year fixed rate. This is probably the shortest term most purchasers will undertake; your payments will be much higher than a thirty-year mortgage and higher than a twenty-year mortgage. The payment on this fifteen-year mortgage will be $1,392.36. Principal exceeds interest as early as year four, and you only pay $85,625 in interest. You can build equity fast, assuming your home doesn't depreciate and continues the traditional appreciation.

Fixed-rate mortgages might be a good choice for borrowers who plan to hold on to the home for a long period of time. For borrowers who only plan to own the home for a short period before selling and hope to capitalize on the home's appreciation, an adjustable-rate or an interest-only loan may be an option. They are both very risky and can become costly.

Adjustable-Rate Mortgages (ARM)

Adjustable-rate mortgages come in many different packages, for example, a 5/1, 10/1, 7/1, or 3/1. The first number represents the term of the fixed rate, which is usually lower than the traditional prevailing fixed-rate loans; the second number represents how often the interest rate will adjust. In the case of a 5/1 ARM, the introductory rate is in effect for five years and will adjust once a year for the remaining twenty-five years on a thirty-year mortgage. A 5/5 ARM is a rare find; it adjusts every five years after the initial five-year introductory period, which provides less volatility. Because you can't always predict future market conditions or interest rates, an ARM is very risky. You may plan to buy a home, live in it for only five years, and sell it to capitalize on the appreciation before your mortgage rate adjusts, which will be based on either the US Treasury rate or the London Interbank Offered Rate. You must cross a few hurdles before you can capitalize on the sale. First, your house must appreciate a significant amount to cover the expenses you incurred to purchase the home and the expenses you will incur to sell the home. Second, you are banking on a seller's market condition, one where you are able to sell the home with relative ease. These conditions exist when there are more buyers looking for homes than there are homes on the market.

Adjustable-rate mortgages have caps or maximums on the amount a rate can increase; the cap structure offers some protection against these risky loans. For example, if you have a 3.2 percent interest rate on a 5/1 ARM with a 2-2-8 cap, the first number represents the percentage the loan can possibly increase in year six, and the second number determines the maximum amount in year seven and subsequent years. The third number is the lifetime cap the interest rate can increase over the initial rate. So if the loan uses the US Treasury rate, and it increases 4 percent in year six, your interest rate will not increase more than 2 percent to 5.2 percent, and over the life of the loan, it can never increase more than 8 percent to 11.2 percent, which is pretty expensive.

Look at the example below; it shows the difference in payment for a fixed-rate thirty-year $150,000 loan at 4.5 percent, a twenty-year loan at 4.1

percent, and a fifteen-year loan at 3.8 percent versus an ARM loan rate of 3.2 percent in years one through five, 5.2 percent in year six, and 7.2 percent in year seven.

Purchase	Mortgage	Interest Rate	Term	Payment
$150,000	Fixed rate	4.5	30-year	$760.03
$150,000	Fixed rate	4.1	20-year	$916.89
$150,000	Fixed rate	3.8	15-year	$1,094.56
$150,000	ARM 30-year	3.2	5/1 (years 1–5)	$648.70
$150,000	ARM 30-year	5.2	5/1 (year 6)	$823.67
$150,000	ARM 30-year	7.2	5/1 (year 7)	$1,018.18

Analyzing the chart above, you can conclude that a 2 percent increase in year six to the ARM will increase payments by $175 and an additional $195 in year seven for a total increase of $369.48. In addition, the numbers can go higher before the cap takes effect. You can also conclude that the borrower would be better off had he or she opted for a thirty-year or twenty-year loan, if he or she remains in the home more than five years. Some consumers select the ARM loan because they can save money. Yes, that is true initially. The total amount saved and available for investments on a 5/1 ARM as opposed to a fixed thirty-year loan during the first five years is $111.33 x 60 = $6,680. If you had invested the savings of $111.33 each month for five years, you would have $8,597.16 with an interest rate of 10 percent compounded monthly. That's not enough to justify a $369 increased payment starting in year seven.

If you remain in the house over fifteen years, chances are extremely likely that your loan will reach the maximum cap, and your payments will be very expensive. So why do borrowers gamble with an ARM?

1. An ARM may qualify a borrower for a higher-priced home, or he or she may bank on income increasing substantially by year five or hope to refinance at a lower rate.
2. The thirty-year fixed-rate payment may not be affordable.
3. Savings from an ARM can be used for investing, remember that the smaller the loan, the less you will save. Purchasers of large

mortgages benefit in this situation, so this is a strategy usually utilized by the wealth.

4. In five years, the borrower hopes to sell the home at an appreciated value.

5. The borrower hopes that interest rates will decline or remain the same.

Other Risky Mortgage Loans

- Interest-only loan. Just as the name implies, you only pay the interest on the loan for a specified period of time, usually three to ten years. After the predetermined period, your original mortgage balance remains untouched; in addition, the interest rate will adjust based on the terms of the adjustable-rate mortgage. Let's say, for example, that your interest-only period ends after five years; at this time, you are expected to pay both principal and interest amortized over a twenty-five-year period. This causes your payments to automatically increase, especially with the higher interest rate. The payment can easily increase to an amount you can't afford.

- Subprime loan. If your credit score is worthy, usually above 640, you can get a prime loan with a favorable interest rate. If your score is lower or if you have a poor credit history, your alternative is a subprime loan with a less favorable interest rate; it is an alternative for borrowers who may otherwise not be able to obtain credit. These loans carry high interest rates, protecting the lender in case the borrower defaults.

- Negative amortization loans. This is probably one of the worst loans on the market. It allows you to make a minimum payment that covers some of the principal but not the interest. The unpaid interest and principal are added back to the original loan; consequently, you owe more than the original principal balance. Unless you throw a huge lump-sum payment toward the balance, it is difficult to build equity or retire the debt.

The Mortgage Crisis

In 2006, the housing market was riddled with interest-only, subprime, and negative amortization loans. The foreclosure rates between 2006 and 2007 were at an all-time high. Americans could not afford the payments on their risky loan obligations. The domino effect led to the credit crisis, the gateway to the Great Recession, which lasted from 2007 to 2009, followed by huge declines in home values. Many homeowners who could afford their homes had no equity; they owed more than the home was worth. Some of those homeowners walked away because their homes were no longer a sound investment.

It was easy to blame the debacle on consumers seeking the American dream of owning a home or on government fiscal policy that urged lenders to ease lending requirements for potential home buyers. But other sinister objectives were in play that led to the Great Recession. It began after the stock market crash in the early 2000s, when the US Federal Reserve tried to stimulate the economy by lowering interest rates. For large investors, the interest rates were too low and were unattractive for investing; therefore, they sought other alternatives.

Wall Street provided a solution. They seized the opportunity to obtain low-interest leveraged loans to buy mortgages and sell them. It produced the perfect low-risk investment with a AAA credit rating to offer potential investors, or so they thought. Investment banks such as Goldman Sachs, Morgan Stanley, and JPMorgan Chase purchased these mortgages, packaged them, and sold them to large investors such as mutual-fund and pension-fund investors. They were peddled as collateralized debt obligations (CDOs) that came with low-cost insurance policies called credit default swaps, covering the investor if the homeowner defaulted. The premise was that homes would appreciate and that the investment banks could easily resell the home, eliminating any loss should the homeowner default.

Sounded like a great marriage, so what happened? Greed was a major player; the demand for CDOs was greater than the originating and servicing mortgage bankers could deliver. With a limited supply of qualified home buyers, they reverted to accepting subprime loans from other lenders. Everyone closed their eyes to the fact that these newly attracted home buyers could not afford their loans; some borrowers were actually unemployed.

Many gainfully employed individuals abandoned their jobs to generate subprime mortgage loans. They completed whatever training was necessary to enter into the lucrative mortgage business. They used aggressive tactics, enticing potential borrowers to buy or refinance mortgage loans they couldn't afford. Normally interested home buyers approach a lender when they are ready to buy or refinance a home, but there was so much money to be made that lenders or lenders' representatives were approaching the homeowners and individuals. Many unscrupulous tactics were used to secure loans from unsuspecting buyers.

Mortgage bankers would approve unqualified borrowers with low credit scores and insufficient income in order to make huge amounts in fees, sometimes more than $10,000 per loan. They also enlisted the help of unethical home appraisers, who would value a home at $130,000 when in reality its fair market value was closer to $60,000, in order to qualify the borrower for refinancing. After their shameful excessive fees were collected, the loans were simply sold to the investment banker, who packaged them with the others and sold them to investors. The mortgage lender incurred no risk at all, which was an incentive to approve anyone.

After borrowers began to default on their risky loans and no longer were making payments on their mortgages, the income stream for Wall Street slowed down considerably. Nonpayment led to a flood of homes on the market due to foreclosures, which caused the value of homes in general to plummet.

Some of the investment bankers went bankrupt and were unable to make good on the credit-default-swap insurance; consequently, pensions and mutual funds that included mortgage-backed investments suffered. Now there were millions of foreclosed homes on the market, resulting from loans that borrowers were never able to sustain; in addition, qualified homeowners experienced a large decline in their equity. Major banks began to file for bankruptcy, and that, coupled with losses in retirement investments, created the great mortgage crisis, which led to a bailout costing Americans trillions of dollars because the banks were "too big to fail."

The Consumer Financial Protection Bureau created rules to prevent what happened in the housing bubble from happening again. A lender must now verify that borrowers can repay their loan obligations, which requires verification of employment, credit score rating, and debt-to-income ratios.

The New Qualified Mortgage Rules

Effective in 2014, qualified mortgage rules have toughened the requirements for home ownership, but on the other hand, these rules protect consumers from unfair and fraudulent practices, and lenders can't promote interest-only loans, negative amortization loans, or balloon loans. In addition, lenders can't charge you more than 3 percent of the loan amount for points and fees. These rules offer protection, but you have to do your part as well. In order to qualify, you'll need

- a good credit score, a minimum of 620 to 640;
- verifiable income and assets; and
- a debt-to-income ratio of 43 percent or less.

When you are ready to buy a home, you should shop for the mortgage first; lenders can provide you with the maximum home purchase you can afford using a prequalifying model. Use this information to save time by only shopping for homes within your price point. When choosing a home, you should consider future needs and lifestyles. If you buy a condo, budget for condo fees, and consider the ease or complexity you may have selling your condo if you outgrow it. Manufactured homes (mobile homes) depreciate in value over a period of time as opposed to appreciating. They usually require 20 percent down payment and have a shorter finance period with higher interest rates.

Some home buyers enter into uncomfortable loans with the anticipation that income will rise or that they won't incur any unexpected major expenses in the short term. Don't bite off more than you can chew. A mortgage that is too big will leave you less money for savings, investments, retirement, vacations, and college funds. Too big of a mortgage will also leave you vulnerable to foreclosure and bankruptcy. Always review your goals, and go with your gut feeling. Save enough money to cover routine expenses for at least six months. In addition, save a substantial amount for a down payment to avoid the additional expense of mortgage insurance. If your down payment is less than 20 percent of the appraised value or sales price, your monthly payment will be more.

Elements of a Mortgage Payment

Principal. The principal is the net amount of money borrowed from a lender to purchase a home, which consists of the sales price minus your down payment plus any other expenses you finance; repayment is usually paid monthly based on the terms of the loan.

Interest. The interest is the amount of money charged for the loan based on current market conditions and your credit score.

Taxes. Taxes are the payment based on the value of the home assessed by the county and usually collected monthly and held in escrow by the lender until payment is required by the county in which you live.

Homeowners insurance. The lender for your mortgage will require that you have sufficient insurance to cover any catastrophic incident, such as a fire or flood. Shop around for a premium that provides replacement value of your home in case it is completely destroyed.

Mortgage insurance. This insurance protects the lender in case the borrower defaults on the loan. The lower the borrower's down payment, the higher the risk to the lender. Premiums are paid on mortgage balances less than 80 percent loan-to-value ratio. Once your loan-to-value ratio reaches 78 percent, contact the lender to have your mortgage insurance canceled.

After you have found the home of your dreams, perhaps with the assistance of a real estate agent, you will sign a contract expressing your commitment to buy and the owner's commitment to sell. Your real estate agent is instrumental in this process and should have your best interests in mind, as the selling agent has the seller's interests in mind.

The Loan Process

- Loan application fee. A small fee is collected by the lender to check your credit and retrieve your credit score to analyze his or her risk. The fee may be credited toward loan closing costs.
- Earnest money. After the seller accepts an offer from the buyer, the home is taken off the market. The seller loses the opportunity to market the home to anyone else, in which case the seller may request earnest money from the buyer. The amount is usually between $500 and $1,000, representing good faith. If you are not serious about your offer, don't commit to the payment, because it is not refundable simply because you changed your mind. There are other circumstances where you can receive a refund, for example, if you don't qualify for the loan or the home inspection reveals unsatisfactory conditions. If you do proceed with the purchase of the property, earnest money will be credited toward closing costs associated with the loan.
- Home inspection. Most lenders require a home inspection; if they don't, you should consider obtaining one for your benefit. You could discover that the house you are interested in is not structurally sound. For this reason, you can and should rescind the transaction. You can expect to pay $200 to $450 for a home inspection.
- Pest inspection. An inspection can identify any pest problems, and the professional you use to conduct the inspection will probably offer you a treatment plan requiring recurring payments. Pests that can infest the home run the gamut; however, the ones that cause the most

serious trouble are termites. They are a constant threat to your home. Daniel R. Suiter, PhD, at the University of Georgia Department of Entomology, says that termites are found in every state except Alaska, probably due to the frigid temperatures that prevail all year there. Termites are capable of penetrating wood, plaster, metal siding, and more. If termites go undetected and untreated, they can render your home structurally unsound; it's worth the average $200 fee and a protection plan.

You can expect to shore up or finance the following expenses at closing:

- Down payment—The new qualified mortgage rules don't identify a minimum down payment amount, keeping the door open for first-time home buyers who may not be able to raise 10 percent of the home price. Be prepared to pay between 3 percent and 10 percent down.
- Closing cost—These expenses should not exceed 3 percent of the mortgage balance; they usually include attorney's fees, loan origination fees, points, appraisal fees, and several other expenses connected to the loan and your home.
- Mortgage insurance premium / private mortgage insurance— If your down payment is less than 20 percent of the appraised value, you will pay monthly mortgage insurance premiums for an FHA loan or monthly private mortgage insurance for a private conventional loan until your loan-to-value ratio reaches 78 percent. You can expect to pay an amount between 0.3 percent and 1.35 percent of the original loan amount, depending on the size of your down payment and the loan. A higher down payment decreases lenders' risk; they believe that the more skin you have in the game, the less likely you are to default. In addition to the monthly premiums, you may be required to pay an up-front mortgage insurance premium on an FHA loan, about 2.25 percent of the base loan up front, or you may be able to finance it.

Renting

If you can't afford a house right now but are anxious to move out on your own, renting would be the next logical step. You first want to decide where you want to live. Some things to consider are how safe the area is and how convenient it is to your job, family, friends, banks, shopping, and so on. Decide what is most important to you when you choose a location. You can find available rentals in your area of interest and price range by utilizing the local paper, free rental guides, word of mouth, and local advertisements. Don't shop in a hurry; look for advertised move-in specials.

Your rental application will help landlords decide if you are a good risk. The landlord will complete a credit check and verify employment and salary. Once you have been checked out, you will be asked to sign the lease. The lease states the terms or the agreement; make sure you read it and understand it. The terms specify the monthly rental amount, late fees, whether pets are allowed, and the conditions for receiving your security deposit back. The lease will also tell you the consequences of terminating your lease early. In addition, it can tell you about rental increases for future renewals.

Before moving in you can expect to pay the following:

- first month's rent
- last's month's rent
- deposit for gas, electric, and water, if your credit score is low
- security deposit
- renter's insurance
- application fee

After you have moved in, you can expect to pay the agreed-upon rental payment each month, usually by the first of the month and no later than the fifth; otherwise you will be charged a late-payment fee. You will also have utility payments—gas, electric, and water. These are all basic expenses. Other expenses may include telephone, cable, and Internet.

CHAPTER 7

Protecting Your Assets and Income

After you have built your wealth, you should take steps to protect it by minimizing loss from risk exposure. A long-term stay in the hospital can bankrupt you if you don't have the proper health-insurance coverage. Your family can experience a loss of income after a catastrophic event such as death or disability if you haven't taken the proper steps to minimize risk. Unfortunately, it's easy to ignore the possibility that a disastrous event could happen to you and create a financial hardship in your life.

Evaluate your needs to determine the type and amount of insurance you should have. It's impossible to eliminate all risk, but you can certainly minimize it. The most common types of insurance that can protect you or provide supplemental income are life insurance, health insurance, disability insurance, homeowners insurance, and automobile insurance.

Health Insurance

Health insurance insures you against the risk of incurring medical expenses you may not be able to pay out of pocket. If your employer offers a policy, you should consider it if it meets your needs and you can afford it. Often employers pay a portion of your premium, and with large companies you get the benefit of group coverage that often includes a discount. If there is no health insurance offered by your employer or you can't afford the insurance offered, you can shop for affordable insurance in the marketplace under the Affordable Care Act (ACA), which was enacted on March 23, 2010; open enrollment in the health-care marketplace began October 2013. Beginning in 2014, the ACA goal is to provide all Americans with affordable health-insurance options. Many middle- and low-income Americans who previously could not afford insurance are provided credits under the new law, making insurance affordable.

Automobile Insurance

Don't drive without it. A car accident can be costly, robbing you of not only your investment in your automobile but also other assets you have accumulated if you are sued. Consider obtaining insurance that protects you financially from property damage, medical bills, legal fees, and loss of income. You want protection from motorists that cause damage to your car and are uninsured and unable to repair your vehicle. You also want coverage in case you cause damages to other vehicles, individuals, or property. A good automobile policy also covers your vehicle due to theft or vandalism.

For young adults under the age of twenty-five, the premiums can be expensive because drivers under that age usually are inexperienced, which increases the risk of accidents, especially if they drive a small, fast car. The insurance companies know this and charge a higher premium rate for young drivers. High insurance rates can derail your budget and keep you from meeting your goals. Driving fast and over the speed limit can lead to speeding tickets, and speeding tickets are factors in higher insurance premiums. Driving under the influence and not obeying traffic laws also makes you a big risk for insurance companies because you have established a pattern of bad driving behavior, which is a precursor to accidents, leading to insurance payments for damages, and, consequently, higher insurance rates for you. Some insurance companies won't take a risk on reckless drivers.

Your automobile choice also affects your premium rate. Bankrate.com said that one of the most expensive cars to insure is a Subaru Impreza WRX 4WD, and one of the least expensive is the Buick Rendezvous four-door. Basically, the cars that younger drivers are attracted to cost more and are usually more expensive to insure than cars that are family sized and that young drivers consider old-fashioned. However, some large vehicles, such as Hummers, may be safer for the driver but cause huge damages to anyone they may collide with; therefore, they are more expensive to insure. Another factor that increases your insurance premium is the car theft rate of the vehicle you drive.

Talk to your insurance agent about the cost to insure your car before you purchase it; where you live, your credit history and your prior driving record will be major factors in determining your premium cost. Sometimes policy holders opt for a higher deductible, which is the amount you, the insured, will pay out of pocket before the insurance company will cover the peril, but that amount may be too high. For example, you have a collision that is your fault, the damages are $900, and your deductible is $1,000. Your premium is cheaper, but can you afford to pay $900 out of pocket?

Collision insurance. This insurance will cover the repair or replacement of your vehicle after a collision with another vehicle or object. There is usually a deductible before the insurance company will cover your loss. This insurance coverage may be optional in your state unless you are leasing or financing your vehicle. But you will carry the entire risk.

Liability insurance. This insurance covers bodily injury and property damage to others that you caused during the operation of your vehicle and is required by most states. If you are at fault, you can be sued. Choose the amount of coverage you carry wisely because the injured party can also seek restitution from you personally if your coverage is not sufficient, which means your home, business, and other assets are at risk. Usually there is not a deductible out-of-pocket amount to meet before payment is made on your behalf.

Comprehensive insurance. Conversely, comprehensive insurance covers damage to your vehicle that is not caused by a collision; it usually includes theft, vandalism, storm damage, or other acts against your vehicle. Normally, there is a deductible amount that you must meet before payment is made. If a tree limb falls on your car and causes damages of $800 and your deductible is $1,000, your insurance will not reimburse you for any of the damages. The deductible is per occurrence. Likewise, if your car is stolen and is worth $1,000, you won't receive anything from your insurance. In this case, you may consider not carrying comprehensive insurance or opting for a lower deductible. Reports show that a car is stolen in America every 43.7 seconds and that the Honda Accord was the top stolen car in 2012 and 2013; insurance prices will reflect those statistics. Owning a turquoise car verses a black car can save you money; black cars tend to be stolen more and turquoise cars much, much less.

There are also insurance options to protect your property from uninsured or underinsured motorists and to cover your bodily injuries. Medical coverage pays for medical expenses regardless of who is at fault. If you have good medical-insurance coverage, it may not be necessary to have double coverage. There are options to purchase rental-car reimbursement and roadside assistance. Weigh the premium cost and the coverage it provides.

I suggest that you shop around at least every two years; don't get too complacent with your insurance company and assume they are offering you the best deal. I remained loyal to my insurance carrier for over twenty years, and the carrier thanked me every year by continuously raising my premium. I finally realized that the yearly increases were based on my willingness to pay and not shop for better coverage. I decided to do some comparison shopping—a dreaded, time-consuming task. I compared coverage and found that I was able to reduce my cost by 40 percent for the same coverage.

Apparently the longer you've been with a company, the more you will save when you switch, because you've been subjected to many years of loyalty increases. Some industries reward their long-term customers, but automobile insurers are not one of them. If the insurance company thinks you won't switch, they may optimize your premium. The company may gather information about you online, including social media and your shopping habits to determine if you will remain loyal or switch. Based on the proprietary formula fueled by the information the company gathers, you may be categorized as stable and unlikely to switch in spite of higher premiums. It's a nasty strategy that the insurance companies have been able to use by circumventing the consumer-protection laws that are designed to ensure fair pricing of insurance products to the public.

Homeowners Insurance

This insurance coverage will replace or repair your home and its contents after an incident such as a fire or flood. Don't cut corners; choose options that will adequately cover your loss. For example, it's cheaper to choose cash-value reimbursement as opposed to replacement value. Consider a scenario where you purchase a home for $200,000 and currently have an outstanding debt of $160,000; however, with so many homes in foreclosure status in your neighborhood, your home's value has declined and is appraised at only $150,000. Your home is destroyed by a fire, so you file a claim and receive the cash value of $150,000 based on your current value, minus a $2,000 deductible. The cost of building material and labor has increased since your original purchase, but you don't have enough to replace the home; in fact, you owe the lien holder $10,000.

Renter's Insurance

Renter's insurance is usually required by the landlord who rents an apartment or home to you. Renter's insurance covers your possessions within the dwelling unit from fire, floods, theft, and vandalism. The landlord usually carries coverage for the overall dwelling unit.

Disability Insurance

Disability insurance protects your income, savings, and investments in the event you become disabled. Wikipedia defines disability as the consequences of an impairment that may be physical, cognitive, mental, sensory, emotional, developmental, or some combination of the above. Long-term and short-term benefits are available for purchase. Disability insurance can be expensive, probably because Social Security statistics predict that over one in four twenty-year-olds will become disabled before they retire.

Disability insurance is valuable but not as popular as the others mentioned. I once read an article about two very successful lawyers with countless lavish material possessions, including a million-dollar home and luxury cars. While traveling together after a successful business trip, they were involved in a car accident that left them both totally disabled. The couple had been wise enough to obtain life insurance, health insurance, and automobile insurance, which covered the initial medical bills and replaced the automobile. I'm sure that they had more than enough in assets to cover their living expenses for an extended period of time. However, the couple didn't plan for permanent disability, leaving them with an uncovered risk. They eventually sold their home to cover living expenses and the mounting medical expenses once the insurance payments met their medical lifetime limits; they watched as their wealth slowly dwindled away.

Life Insurance

Life insurance is pushed in front of you from the time you are born and onward. Have you heard of the Gerber Life Grow Up Plan? They air commercials, mail flyers to new parents, and have brochures prominently placed in doctors' offices. But what you may not have known is that the Grow Up Plan is nothing more than life insurance and is a bad investment, in my opinion. The company up-sells the product by baiting you with the fact that the money you contribute to this plan can be used later in life to help fund education or emergencies for your child. However, there are better options—for example, the Coverdale Educational Savings Account, the Uniform Gift to Minors Act or Uniform Transfers to Minors Act (UGMA/UTMA), and the Education 529 Plan.

If someone tells you that life insurance is a great investment for children, run the other way. Nevertheless, let's first talk about who needs life insurance. In order to understand who needs life insurance, we need a better understanding of the purpose of life insurance. Life insurance is a product that you purchase in order to protect your loved ones in case something were to happen to you. When I refer to loved ones, I mean anyone depending on your income, whether it's your spouse, children, or any other dependents. When asking yourself whether you need to purchase life insurance, ask yourself, Will anyone suffer a financial hardship if I die?

Some employers offer free life insurance; it is usually the amount of your salary up to $50,000. Any life insurance premiums paid by your employer over the $50,000 coverage limit is usually included as additional income to you, and you will have to claim it on your tax return and pay taxes on it. If you are offered free life insurance from your employer as part of your benefits package but currently don't have any loved ones depending on your income, you should still take it; it's free. I just wouldn't recommend going out and purchasing additional coverage until you need it.

The world of life insurance can get quite complex; some of the different options and policy riders can be a big rip-off with fancy names, and some are very simple and serve the intended purpose. The four main types of life insurance are term life, whole life, universal life, and variable life.

Term Life Insurance

Term life is a protection policy where you select the term (number of years you want to be covered) and the amount of insurance coverage you need. The provider will ask you many personal questions in order to get a quote on how much you will pay in monthly premiums for coverage.

Some factors make your premium expensive, including your age, whether you smoke or engage in risky activities or have a risky job, and whether you have preexisting medical conditions (diabetes, high blood pressure, etc.). Basically, the healthier you are, the cheaper it is to afford life insurance. The typical term for term life insurance is twenty years, about the amount of time needed to raise your children and reach the end of your mortgage payment with lots of equity. If one spouse were to die while the couple owed a large sum on their house and while their children were young, the resulting burden could financially break the surviving spouse. There are also other term lengths available, ranging from five to thirty-five years. Term life insurance does an excellent job in providing financial protection during the time you are financially exposed.

Now the remaining three options—whole life, universal life, and variable life—are all investment policies. If you haven't been approached by someone telling you that one of these investment options is the best thing since sliced bread, then just wait for it, because it's coming. I've met insurance salespeople who have made a fortune selling this stuff at your expense. Whole life, universal life, and variable life insurance options are also known as permanent life insurance. Unlike term life insurance, the coverage is for the remainder of your life. The premiums on these policies are significantly higher than a term life policy because you pay extra money for investments.

Whole Life Insurance

People gravitate toward these plans because the insurance company sells them on the idea that they will earn a return on investment with the ability to withdraw money from the policy. There is one caveat; it must be repaid.

But here's the major disadvantage to the investment portion and the cash-value part; you don't get any say in how your money is invested, so you can't really be guaranteed that the cash value will grow.

Would you hand over half a million dollars to a company and say, "Here, invest as you wish, and whatever you tell me the profit is, I'll take it"? The insurance companies can make huge profits on these policies. And once again, what was the point of the insurance policy?

Universal Life Insurance (UL)

Universal life (UL) is similar to whole life in terms of investing part of your premiums. Usually, UL insurance guarantees a minimum of 4 percent in returns. If it has been a bullish year for the insurance company, for example, earning a whopping 12 percent return on their investments, there is no guarantee that you will earn the same. You can make smart decisions about investing your own money instead of paying for an overpriced life-insurance policy with the promise of receiving earnings thirty years later that may not have outpaced inflation.

Variable Life Insurance

Variable life insurance is classified as a security and falls under the regulation of the federal securities laws, and there's no guarantee on how well the extra money you pay for investments will perform. This is probably the most risky of the four options. If your investments are not performing well, your monthly required premium could skyrocket in order to cover the original premium. You also cannot borrow from the cash value. So in short, you are better off creating an investment fund of your own and picking your own investments if you are going to assume the risk of a variable-life-insurance policy.

There are also insurance riders that you can purchase as add-ons to your basic policy. They are often expensive and probably benefit the insurance company more than you.

CHAPTER 8

Plan for Retirement

Believe it or not, one day your body will grow tired of punching the clock every day and competing with new technology and the next generation. You will want to start the next chapter of your life, which does not include the daily grind. But what if you're not ready financially? Thirty years ago, when workers reached the retirement age of sixty-five, they received a gold watch and a comfortable monthly payment from their employers' guaranteed pension plans, with little contributions or planning on their part. That was when defined benefit plans were popular and affordable.

Employers used a calculation based on salary and years of service to determine a worker's monthly defined benefits for life.

Not many employers are funding defined benefit plans today because those plans have become an albatross, with long-term expensive funding and payments that can reduce a company's bottom line. Instead, more employers are funding defined contribution plans. Under these types of plans, the employer may contribute a monetary portion or may match your contribution up to a certain percentage. You are not guaranteed a defined payment; you have to rely upon the timing, the size of your contributions, good investment decisions, and good market conditions to earn enough to receive comfortable monthly income payments for life.

Start early putting away money, allowing time to increase the value of your investment; time adds value to a good, sound investment. Americans are living longer, which requires more income. Don't you want to have the time and the money you've saved to do the things you've always wanted to do? Have you calculated how much money you will need to do this? Some analysts say that you'll need 70 to 80 percent of your income today to live a similar lifestyle in retirement.

401(k) Retirement Plan

The 401(k) is a type of defined contribution plan that employees in the workforce today are more likely to be offered, if the employer offers a retirement plan at all. You may need to pass a probationary period before you are eligible to participate. Once that period is over, you should contribute to your employer's plan at least up to the employer's match; otherwise you are giving up free money.

The amount you earn depends on the investments you make; there are no guarantees of how well your investments will do. The funds you choose to invest in are usually managed by a fund manager, to whom you pay a small management fee. You will also receive a tax break because your contributions to the plan and its earnings are deferred from income until you withdraw the money at retirement. The maximum pretax contribution for the year 2015 is $18,000.

You can actually contribute to this type of retirement plan at a discount. Let's say you are considering making a $150 contribution monthly. If you decide not to make the contribution and your taxable rate falls into the 15 percent tax bracket, the tax you will owe on $150 each month is $22.50. If you actually make the contribution of $150, it will save you $22.50 each month on taxes if the entire amount qualifies for deferment. The higher the tax bracket, the deeper the discount. Tax on $150 for anyone in the 28 percent tax bracket equals $42; you'll be making the contribution at a discount of only $108. You saved $42 because the entire amount is excluded from income.

Roth IRA

If your employer does not offer a retirement plan at work, consider making contributions to a Roth IRA. Contributions are not deferred, and there are no tax deductions for your contribution. Anyone of any age can make a contribution as long as he or she has qualified compensation. A good strategy is to contribute to your employer's defined contribution plan up to the match and contribute any additional funds to a Roth up to the maximum. You will avoid leaving free money on the table and benefit with tax-free earnings from the Roth.

You can withdraw original ontributions from a Roth at any time tax free and penalty free. You can withdraw your earnings tax and penalty-free, if you have had the Roth account for at least five tax years and meet one of the exceptions. Some of those exceptions include using the money for medical purposes, education, disability, or for a first-time home purchase. You can also withdraw penalty- and tax-free after reaching the age of fifty-nine and a half. You should start the Roth IRA as soon as possible. For the 2015 tax year, contributions are generally limited to $5,500 or your taxable compensation, whichever is less. If you are over the age of fifty, contributions cap at $6,500 or taxable compensation, whichever is less. You can split the contributions between a Roth and traditional IRA with the same contribution limits. There are income limits that limit or disallow contributions. See IRS's publication 590-A for details.

Traditional IRA

The traditional IRA works much the same as the Roth, except you may be able to take a partial or full deduction against income, which may reduce taxable income. The deduction is based largely on whether you are covered by a retirement plan at work and your income. IRS publication 590-A reports the limits based on inflation each year.

Don't put money in a retirement plan that you will need before retirement. There are stiff penalties for early withdrawal, that is, before you reach the age of fifty-nine and a half, unless you meet one of the exceptions. If you take an early distribution, you will receive 20 percent less because 20 percent is automatically withheld to cover anticipated taxes. If you have income that falls into the 28 percent tax bracket, you may have a hefty tax bill, especially after you add the 10 percent early-withdrawal penalty. There are exceptions to the penalty but not the tax. A distribution usually puts you in a higher tax bracket, which equates to higher taxes; if left unpaid, the IRS charges penalties and interest. Consequently, your early payout is less.

To avoid the early-withdrawal penalty and taxes, some employees borrow money from their employer-offered retirement plan as opposed to taking a distribution. This act is permitted; however, it has its financial and tax consequences as well. When you take money out of your retirement fund, that's less money earning money; in addition, when you pay back the money, you are paying it back with dollars that are taxed, and you will be taxed again when you withdraw it in retirement. In essence, you will be paying tax on the same dollars twice. Moreover, if you fail to pay the loan in full, you will be taxed at your tax rate and charged a 10 percent penalty for early withdrawal.

Retirement Savings Contribution Credit

You may be able to take advantage of the IRS Retirement Savings Contribution Credit if you are a low to moderate-income worker. It offsets part of the first eligible $2,000 you contribute to your retirement plan or IRA. This credit is in addition to any other credit that may apply. The credit is 50 percent, 20 percent, or 10 percent of your retirement contribution, depending on adjusted gross income. The maximum credit is $2,000 for a single filer or $4,000 for married couples filing jointly. For 2015, the credit is phased out for married couples filing jointly when adjusted gross income is more than $61,000, head of household filers, more than $45,750 and for all other filers, adjusted gross income can't exceed $30,500. The income limits are adjusted each year for inflation. A few caveats—you must be at least eighteen years old, not be a full-time student, and can't be claimed as a dependent on someone else's tax return. This new credit eliminates the excuse that you don't earn enough money to contribute toward your retirement.

Example

A single qualified filer with total earnings from wages of $18,000 can contribute $1,000 to a qualifying retirement plan and reduce his or her tax liability by $500, based on adjusted gross income.

$1,000 x .50 = $500

The credit is against tax and is non-refundable.

Exercise

Mary begins her career in 2012 at the age of twenty-four with a beginning salary of $30,000 a year. Her employer does not offer a retirement plan. She chooses to contribute to a Roth IRA account. The figures do not include inflation adjustments.

Scenario 1

If Mary contributes a lump sum of $5,000 to her Roth account at the beginning of the year in 2012 and contributes the same at the beginning of years 2013 and 2014, earning an average 10 percent return, and never contributes again, how much will she have twenty-seven years later? $230,735.

Scenario 2

How much will she have if she first contributes $5,000 at the beginning of year sixteen and contributes the same amount for the next fourteen years before retirement at the same rate of return? $174,749.

Scenario 3

How much will she have if she contributes $5,000 at the beginning of every year for thirty years at the same rate of return? $904,717.

It is important to contribute early; time is a powerful ally. Scenario 3 is the perfect example of how Mary can retire at age fifty-four with near-millionaire status after thirty years in the workforce. Scenario 1 shows how contributing a small amount early outperforms scenario 2; although more money is invested, it has less time to grow.

Exercise

Charlestene earned $42,000 in 2014; she has the standard 10 percent federal tax withheld from her gross income—$4,200. She participated in an employer's 401(k) plan for over five years, at which time she became fully vested in her plan, with withdrawal rights. Charlestene's taxable income after her exemption of $3,900 and standard deduction of $6,100 is $32,000 before the withdrawal. She is single with no dependents. Charlestene withdrew $8,000 from her retirement plan for a dream vacation. What is Charlestene's federal tax liability before the withdrawal? How much with the $8,000 withdrawal?

Rate	Single filer
10%	$0 to $8,925 +
15%	$8,925 to $36,250 +
25%	$36,250 to $87,850 +

Using the marginal tax brackets above, Charlestene's tax without the withdrawal is calculated below:

$8,925 x 10% = $895.50 +
$23,075 x 15% = $3,461.25
Total tax = $4,356.75

Using the marginal tax brackets above, Charlestene's tax with the $8,000 withdrawal is calculated below:

$8,925 x 10% = $895.50 +
$27,325 x 15% = $4,098.75 +
$3,750 x 25% = $937.50
Total tax = $5,931.25 + $800 (10% penalty) = $6,731.25

Early withdrawal from a retirement account can cost you a substantial amount in taxes. In addition to the taxes, you are assessed a 10 percent penalty. It's a good idea to find other ways to finance a vacation. Early withdrawal has cost Charlestene an extra $2,374.50; that's 30 percent of the initial withdrawal. Unfortunately, this is only half of the story; if she lives in a state that levies state income tax, she could pay even more.

Other Retirement Plans

Other retirement vehicles include the 403(b) offered to school system employees, the Savings Incentive Match Plan for Employees (SIMPLE) is used by small-employer-based retirement plans, and the Employee Stock Ownership Plan (ESOP) allows employees to invest in the company's stock and own a part of the company. Simplified Employee Pension (SEP) plans are used by small employers and self-employed persons.

CHAPTER 9

Estate Planning

Benjamin Franklin once said, "In this world nothing can be said to be certain, except death and taxes." You know about paying taxes while you are living and working, but did you know that you can be taxed after you die? Although death and taxes are certain, you can plan to make estate taxes less burdensome to your loved ones.

Estate Taxes

The IRS defines estate tax as a tax on your right to transfer property at your death. You may be required to pay tax on your gross estate. In computing your gross estate, the fair market value of everything you own at the time of death is considered. The fair market value is the amount a willing buyer would pay to a willing seller in the marketplace.

The IRS allows you to transfer some of your assets free from taxes; this amount is called an exemption. The exemption allows you to exclude a certain amount from the gross estate, effectively reducing your tax liability. In 2013, Congress and President Obama enacted the American Taxpayer Relief Act, which made the exclusion permanent at $5 million indexed for inflation; the remaining amount is subject to an estate tax with a top rate of 40 percent. The American Taxpayer Relief Act also permanently made the federal estate tax exemption portable; that is, a deceased spouse can pass on any unused exemption to the spouse by making the election on federal form 706. Unfortunately, states that levy estate taxes have not adopted the portability clause.

If you are an astute planner, you can also reduce estate taxes while you are living by giving gifts from your estate. You can make gifts yearly to any number of people throughout your life, and if the gifts value $14,000 or less per year, per individual (as of 2015), your exclusion will not be reduced. Amounts given over $14,000 to a single individual in any year reduce the exclusion amount. If you give a gift over $14,000 to someone other than your spouse, you are required to file a gift tax return F-709. There are a few exceptions to the filing requirement and reduction in exclusion; for example, gifts to charity or the direct payment for educational expenses over the limit will not trigger a filing requirement.

Even if your estate doesn't reach $5 million, you must consider your state law. States levy estate taxes as well and offer exclusions that are much less than the federal amount. In addition, seven states levy an inheritance tax, and two states, Maryland and New Jersey, collect both.

Plan for how your wealth will be distributed after death and avoid unnecessary taxes with estate planning; it's not just for the very wealthy. When you include your home, investments, retirement savings, death benefits of a life-insurance policy, interest in a business, vehicles, jewelry, and collectibles, you may be surprised at your net worth.

- Inventory everything you own jointly and separately.
- Assign a value to each asset.
- Create a balance sheet.

Personal Balance Sheet

Assets

Home - Fair Market Value (FMV)	$220,000	
Car FMV	$10,000	
Investments	$60,000	
Cash	$3,000	
Furniture FMV	$15,000	
Stamp collection FMV	$3,000	
Total net assets		$311,000

Liabilities

Mortgage loan	$150,000	
Car loan balance	$7,000	
Student-loan balance	$8,000	
Credit card balance	$2,500	
Installment loan balance	$2,000	
Total liabilities		$169,500

Total net worth $141,500

Last Will and Testament

A will is a legal document that gives you autonomy to determine how you want your property and assets distributed after you die. If you die intestate, that is, without a will, your state determines how your property and assets are distributed; the laws vary from state to state. It's a good idea to research your state law and decide the disposition of your assets in a will.

You may not think that you have enough net worth to expend the time or expense to write your last will and testament, but everyone needs a will. You can eliminate costly legal expenses to determine how assets should be distributed, not to mention disagreements among your heirs if you didn't discuss your intentions prior to death.

What constitutes a legal will varies from state to state. In the state of Georgia, as long as you are over the age of eighteen, of sound mind and body, and the written will is witnessed by at least two qualified witnesses, your will is deemed legal. A notary is not required, and you are not restricted from handwriting your will. Other states may require that your will be typewritten, witnessed, and notarized. This makes the will easy to read and confirms that everyone has seen and signed the will, removing any doubt as to the authenticity of the will and the signatures. Beneficiaries are usually restricted from acting as witnesses for the will; if they do so, they may lose their right to receive any benefits.

Most wills are simple to write; the marketplace provides inexpensive do-it-yourself options to help you create a will without an attorney. However, you should seek the advice of an attorney who specializes in estate planning if you have complex situations, for example, if you have more than one marriage with children or you wish to establish a trust.

If you have young children, you can name a guardian for them in your will. Otherwise, the state may not select the guardian you would have selected. It's a good idea to name an executor, someone that you know and trust, or the state will appoint one for you. An executor is responsible for carrying out or executing the instructions in a will. The executor is also responsible for safeguarding your assets, paying creditors, distributing assets from your estate according to the will, and paying taxes. Executors usually receive a reasonable fee for their services.

Basic elements of a will:

- name and place of residence
- names of spouse, children, and other beneficiaries, such as charities or friends
- alternate beneficiaries
- description of specific gifts
- establishment of a trust
- name of an executor
- name of a guardian(s)
- your signature
- witnesses' signatures

Probate

A will usually goes through probate; the word *probate* means to "prove." A probate court, or some other court of equity, will adjudicate the validity of a will, distribute the assets described in the will, and enforce any provisions or restrictions specified. The probate court also distributes property equitably for those who die intestate. Depending upon the state in which you reside, the complexity of the will, and the location of all parties involved, including the beneficiaries, the probate process may take a few days or many, many months. Probating assets comes with a cost; you can expect to pay court fees, personal representative fees, attorney fees, accounting fees, appraisal fees, bond fees, and a host of other miscellaneous fees that can eat up as much as 10 percent of the value of the deceased's assets before estate taxes and inheritance taxes are paid, if applicable.

Although each state has its laws in dividing property, in general if you die intestate, succession will only include a spouse or a recognized domestic partner and blood relatives. This means friends and charitable organizations are not considered.

Trusts

Trusts are valuable estate-planning tools; a trust is a written document that allows you to place conditions on how and when your assets are distributed. Most estate planners use them to reduce estate and gift taxes and to distribute assets to beneficiaries without the delay and cost of probate court. Trusts vary in types, depending on what the trust maker wishes to accomplish; however, they all contain three key parties.

- The trust maker creates and usually funds the trust with assets and structures the agreement and is often referred to as the trustor or grantor.
- The trustee is responsible for managing the assets titled to the trust.
- The beneficiary receives the benefits of the assets titled to the trust.

Revocable Trust

If the trust is revocable, the trust maker, trustee, and beneficiary are usually the same person, since the assets are solely owned by the living trust maker. This type of trust is also called a living trust because it covers the trust maker while alive and of sound mind and body, allowing the trust maker the management, investment, and benefits from the trust. The trust maker owns all assets and therefore pays taxes on taxable income as an individual on form 1040. In addition, a revocable trust covers provisions in the event the trust maker becomes mentally incapacitated; it contains provisions to name a successor to take over the management of the trust.

When the trust maker dies, the trust becomes irrevocable. The successor trustee takes on the responsibility of paying the trust maker's outstanding bills, debts, and taxes. The remaining amount is distributed to the beneficiaries.

A revocable trust avoids probate court and its expenses because the trustee distributes the assets without the interference of the court. The downside is that this type of trust is unable to protect assets from lawsuits or estate and inheritance taxes.

Irrevocable Trust

Generally this type of trust can't be changed after it is signed by the trust maker. The trust maker gives up ownership of assets to the trustee and beneficiaries. The trust maker is not the trustee but can receive financial benefits from the trust. Benefits include the ability to shield assets from creditors and lawsuits, and this kind of trust is often used to reduce estate taxes.

Because an irrevocable trust is a separate legal entity from the trust maker, the trustee is responsible for filing the federal fiduciary tax return form, 1041 to report income, expenses and liabilities of the trust.

Power of Attorney

A very important element of planning your estate includes establishing power of attorney. This legal document will allow someone to carry out specific or broad acts or actions on your behalf. That person becomes your agent and can sign contracts and checks, withdraw money, and complete other legal acts on your behalf. The agent is not required to be an actual attorney. The problem with a standard power of attorney is that it becomes void after death or the loss of mental clarity. I recommend a durable power of attorney; it remains valid under all mental or physical circumstances. It remains valid after death, allowing the agent the ability to handle estate planning and other financial matters.

Property Ownership

Sole ownership: If you are the sole owner of property, usually probate is necessary to get the property into the hands of your heirs when you die.

Joint ownership:

- Joint tenancy with the right of survivorship (JTWROS). An arrangement where real estate is owned with other individuals. A sale can't take place without the permission of all owners. Upon your death, your portion automatically reverts to the other owners without the need for probate. You don't have a say in naming your beneficiaries. Each owner has equal rights; therefore, a banking account with this type of ownership allows all to withdraw money without the permission of the others.
- Tenancy by the entirety. Usually this arrangement is exclusively between a husband and wife. In order to sell, permission from both parties is necessary. Upon death, the surviving spouse is automatically vested without the need for probate. With bank accounts, it is permissible to withdraw funds without the permission of the other spouse.
- Community property. The community property states are California, Arizona, Idaho, Louisiana, Nevada, New Mexico, Texas, Washington, and New Mexico. This ownership is exclusively for husband and wife. The laws of the state determine ownership.
- Tenancy in common. Unlike a JTWROS, each owner has a specified share and can sell his or her share without permission of the other owners, and upon death, his or her share of the property passes to the beneficiaries and not to the common owner(s).

Exercise

Mr. and Mrs. Smith lived at 50 Peach Street, Mountain, Georgia. Mr. Smith dies in 2009. Mr. and Mrs. Smith owned their home as joint tenants with the right of survivorship. The current Mrs. Smith is the second wife and not the mother of Mr. Smith's two children—Mary Louise

Smith, eighteen years old, and Angela Smith, twenty-five years old. Mrs. Smith does have a child from a previous marriage, Amanda Golath, age twenty-three.

Who inherits the home after Mr. Smith dies? Who will inherit the home if Mrs. Smith dies without a will?

The current Mrs. Smith will inherit the home because of the property ownership; she has the right to survivorship. After Mrs. Smith dies, without a will, Mrs. Smith's daughter, Amanda Golath, will inherit the home. Mr. Smith's daughters, Mary Louise and Angela, will not have a claim to their father's home.

CHAPTER 10

Managing Your Taxes

Now that you have accumulated and protected your wealth, let's see how much you owe the piper, also known as Uncle Sam and the tax man. In 1913, the Sixteenth Amendment gave Congress the authority to enact an income tax that assessed a 1 percent tax on income over $3,000 and 7 percent on income of more than $500,000. In 1918, the top rate escalated to 77 percent to fund World War I. After the war, the top rate declined significantly. For the year 2014, the top rate for ordinary income was 39.6 percent.

When you think of taxes, you may think of the infamous case of Al Capone, a nonfiling, notorious gangster. Elliot Ness, a law enforcer, became famous for chasing Al Capone, trying to bring him down for crimes he'd allegedly committed. Elliot Ness thought that his team was untouchable, but in fact, members of his team were bribed by Capone, which I'm sure was a factor in their failure. It was, after all, Chicago, the Roaring Twenties, and everyone wanted money or status; anyone who was anybody had money. But it was Frank Wilson, an IRS employee, who brought Al Capone down for evading taxes on June 5, 1931. From 1925 to 1929, it was determined that Capone owed over $215,000 in taxes. Using a purchasing power calculator, $215,000 would be worth $3,290,000 in 2013. The judge sentenced Capone to eleven years in Cook County Jail. He was later transferred to Atlanta and finally to the Rock, one of the toughest federal prisons in the nation.

The lesson here is to pay your fair share of taxes to avoid hefty IRS interest, penalties, and even jail time. You do, however, have rights. Ten key critical rights from the Taxpayer Bill of Rights are as follows:

- the right to be informed
- the right to quality service
- the right to pay no more than the correct amount of tax
- the right to challenge the IRS's position and be heard
- the right to appeal an IRS decision in an independent forum
- the right to finality
- the right to privacy
- the right to confidentiality
- the right to retain representation
- the right to a fair and just tax system

The tax system has become complicated since 1913. Some critics have called for the return of the flat tax, or a consumption tax, where the taxes are collected when you buy goods or services. Until this happens, many taxpayers find themselves soliciting the assistance of professional tax preparers.

This arena has become polluted with unscrupulous preparers whose interest is to defraud the government at your expense. Some paid preparers manipulate tax-return information to generate excessive refunds for their clients or modify tax returns after the taxpayer signs them to steal the refunds. Some preparers steal taxpayers' identities to create fictitious returns and generate fraudulent refunds. In most cases, the taxpayer pays the price for the erroneous information because each taxpayer is legally responsible for all the information on the tax return even if someone else prepares it. This January 2015 headline is a good example of a preparer with unscrupulous behavior: "Former H&R Block Owner Jailed for ID Theft."

Scenario:

For the tax year 2013, Mary Wilson takes her tax records to a preparer who promises to get her a big refund fast. Mary drops her tax documents off; no other information was exchanged, and the preparer asked no questions. Mary is fine with that because she thinks she has a simple return. Mary's information is below:

Wages—$35,000; federal withholding—$3,500; state taxes—$1,750; Social Security/Medicare—$2,677.

Mary has no dependents, expenses, or deductions. Her tax situation for 2013 should be:

$35,000
($6,100) standard deduction
($3,900) personal exemption
$25,000 taxable income

$3,303 tax ($892+$2,411)
($3,500) federal withholding
$197 refund

However, what Mary doesn't know is that the preparer added an education credit and a fuel tax credit to further reduce Mary's tax, therefore increasing her refund to $2,197. The preparer pockets the difference, and Mary never knows the difference.

Two years later, Mary is audited for the unusual expense of fuel tax credit and the lack of corroboration of the education credit. Mary now owes the government the refund the preparer pocketed plus interest and possibly a 20 percent penalty unless she can show that she was an unwitting participant and was not culpable.

This should motivate you to learn to prepare your own tax return; it's safer and probably more accurate. The IRS has been successful in punishing many unscrupulous preparers, but there are so many more. The IRS's effort to provide oversight and regulations to protect taxpayers was struck down by the *Loving v. IRS* court ruling in January 2013. The ruling sent a devastating blow against the fight to monitor unethical behavior of return preparers. Legislation is now pending that could provide the IRS the much-needed oversight over return preparers.

You can prepare your own tax return; after all, who knows your situation better than you? We will start with the basic premise that all income is taxable unless explicitly exempt and that most expenses related to income production are deductible. Most individuals operate on a cash basis, which means income is includable in the year received and expenses are deductible in the year paid.

Taxable Income

On January 22, 2015, *Bloomberg* reported this story: "The U.S. Tax Court rejected a California woman's attempt to avoid taxes on the $20,000 she received when she donated her eggs for use by infertile couples." All income is taxable unless it is explicitly excluded. The most common types of income are as follows:

1. Compensation—payment for personal services, including salaries, wages, fees, commissions, tips, bonuses, and specialized forms of compensation such as director's fees, jury fees, and marriage fees received by clergymen
2. Business income (net profit)

3. Gains from property sales (there are exclusions and postponements)
4. Interest income (excludes tax-exempt income)
5. Rents and royalties (prepaid rent is includable when received)
6. Dividends—Stock dividends and capital gain dividends from mutual funds generated from the sale of investments in the fund or undistributed capital gains allocated to shareholders by the company.
7. Alimony and separate maintenance payments not child support
8. Pensions and annuities
9. Income from discharge of indebtedness (there are exceptions)
10. Income passed through
11. Prizes, awards, gambling winnings, and treasure finds
12. Illegal income
13. Unemployment compensation
14. Social Security income—Up until 1984 it was nontaxable, 1984–93 up to 50 percent was taxable, and since 1994 up to 85 percent can be taxable based on income and filing status.
15. Insurance proceeds and court awards—In general insurance proceeds and court awards are taxable; two exceptions are accident and health-insurance benefits and the face amount of life insurance.
16. Tax refunds

IRS form 1040 allows you to list these income amounts directly on the form. Most expenses related to these types of income are deductible as miscellaneous itemized deductions on schedule A. Most other types of income and related deductions are reported on special schedules. Schedule B reports interest and dividends. Schedule C lists self-employment income and losses; schedule D reports capital gains and losses from the sale of assets such as stock. Schedule E reports rental income and expenses, and schedule F reports income and expenses from farming. After income and expenses are calculated on these supporting schedules, the net income or loss is carried over to form 1040.

Tax Preparation

Exercise

Review Mary's scenario below, complete her tax return, and create a new budget for her.

Mary Bell
3620 Beaver Street, Apt. 3-B, Atlanta, Georgia 30013
Social Security Number—123-45-6789
Age 25
College graduate—Accounting
Salary—$48,000 a year, paid monthly; she has three years of experience

Mary is single and moved out of her parents' home and rents an apartment for $850 per month. Mary's mother helped her secure an apartment two years ago before she had credit history. Sometimes she is frugal, but when she sees something she wants and it adds value to her life, she buys it. Mary opened a checking account and savings account at National Bank. Her current credit score is 620.

Mary uses public transportation for work, but one day she would like to own a car. A car would mean that Mary could hang out with her friends and do other things she loves to do without the hassle of public transportation. Mary dreams of getting married and starting a family one day and buying a house, either with her spouse or on her own. She is a super worker at the AAA Accounting firm and receives a yearly raise of 3 percent tied to her performance. Mary's employer offers health insurance and a retirement plan. Currently she is not contributing to the company's retirement plan; however, she is saving $100 a month for her future home. At the end of the year she had $1,213, earning $12 in interest with a 2 percent interest rate.

Mary's health-insurance portion is $308 per month, one-third of the premium; her employer pays the other two-thirds. Mary's employer is a small company and does not offer a defined benefit plan but allows employees to contribute to the company's 401(k) plan. The investment in the plan is not tied to the company's stock; she has a variety of investments from which to choose. The company will match 100 percent of the first 5 percent of salary contributed and 50 percent of the next 3 percent contributed. The maximum contribution to the plan each year is 15 percent. Mary has not found the time to set up her contribution account with the personnel department.

Although Mary received used sofas from her parents, she needed other items. She purchased a dining room table and a bedroom set from Greg's, a retailer, with a balance of $1,200 and an interest rate of 21.5 percent; she pays $100 per month on this installment plan. Mary has two revolving retailer cards—Mable's, 22 percent, and Donte's, 22.5 percent—with a balance of $1,900 and $1,000, respectively. Payments are $125 and $100, respectively. She also has a MasterCard, $900 balance, interest rate 12.5 percent; she pays $40 per month. The credit card really came in handy for Mary; she used it to buy her bedding, bathroom, and bedroom decor. Mary also uses the card for entertainment and to purchase her leisure and work attire; she has to look sharp and professional at work. Mary has an outstanding student loan of $8,190. This is her second year of payment at 6 percent interest, and payments are $200 for a five-year term. She paid $485 in interest in 2013.

Mary's tax and other expenses annually and monthly

Federal taxes withheld (single rate)—$4,500 / 12 = $375
State taxes withheld (single rate)—$2,800 / 12 = $233
Social Security (7.65 percent)—$3672 / 12 = $306
Public transportation (per week)—$25.00 x 4.2 = $105
Electric—$80 monthly
Gas—$50 monthly
Water—$20 monthly
Cable—$80 monthly
Food—$75 per week x 4.2 = $315
Coffee—$28 per week (credit card expenditure)
Internet—$44 monthly
Entertainment—$75 (credit card expenditure)
Hair salon—$150 monthly

Complete Mary's 2013 federal tax return

Form **1040A**	Department of the Treasury—Internal Revenue Service **U.S. Individual Income Tax Return** (99)	**2013**	IRS Use Only—Do not write or staple in this space.

Your first name and initial	Last name		OMB No. 1545-0074
			Your social security number
If a joint return, spouse's first name and initial	Last name		Spouse's social security number
Home address (number and street). If you have a P.O. box, see instructions.		Apt. no.	▲ Make sure the SSN(s) above and on line 6c are correct.
City, town or post office, state, and ZIP code. If you have a foreign address, also complete spaces below (see instructions).			**Presidential Election Campaign** Check here if you, or your spouse if filing jointly, want $3 to go to this fund. Checking a box below will not change your tax or refund. ☐ You ☐ Spouse
Foreign country name	Foreign province/state/county	Foreign postal code	

Filing status
Check only one box.

- 1 ☐ Single
- 2 ☐ Married filing jointly (even if only one had income)
- 3 ☐ Married filing separately. Enter spouse's SSN above and full name here. ▶
- 4 ☐ Head of household (with qualifying person). (See instructions.) If the qualifying person is a child but not your dependent, enter this child's name here. ▶
- 5 ☐ Qualifying widow(er) with dependent child (see instructions)

Exemptions

If more than six dependents, see instructions.

- 6a ☐ **Yourself.** If someone can claim you as a dependent, **do not** check box 6a.
- b ☐ **Spouse**
- c **Dependents:**

(1) First name Last name	(2) Dependent's social security number	(3) Dependent's relationship to you	(4) ✔ If child under age 17 qualifying for child tax credit (see instructions)
			☐
			☐
			☐
			☐
			☐
			☐

Boxes checked on 6a and 6b _____
No. of children on 6c who:
• lived with you _____
• did not live with you due to divorce or separation (see instructions) _____
Dependents on 6c not entered above _____

- d Total number of exemptions claimed.

Add numbers on lines above ▶ ☐

Income

Attach Form(s) W-2 here. Also attach Form(s) 1099-R if tax was withheld.

If you did not get a W-2, see instructions.

7	Wages, salaries, tips, etc. Attach Form(s) W-2.	7
8a	**Taxable** interest. Attach Schedule B if required.	8a
b	**Tax-exempt** interest. **Do not** include on line 8a. 8b	
9a	Ordinary dividends. Attach Schedule B if required.	9a
b	Qualified dividends (see instructions). 9b	
10	Capital gain distributions (see instructions).	10
11a	IRA distributions. 11a	11b Taxable amount (see instructions). 11b
12a	Pensions and annuities. 12a	12b Taxable amount (see instructions). 12b
13	Unemployment compensation and Alaska Permanent Fund dividends.	13
14a	Social security benefits. 14a	14b Taxable amount (see instructions). 14b
15	Add lines 7 through 14b (far right column). This is your **total income.** ▶	15

Adjusted gross income

16	Educator expenses (see instructions). 16	
17	IRA deduction (see instructions). 17	
18	Student loan interest deduction (see instructions). 18	
19	Tuition and fees. Attach Form 8917. 19	
20	Add lines 16 through 19. These are your **total adjustments.**	20
21	Subtract line 20 from line 15. This is your **adjusted gross income.** ▶	21

For Disclosure, Privacy Act, and Paperwork Reduction Act Notice, see separate instructions. Cat. No. 11327A   Form **1040A** (2013)

Form 1040A (2013)

Tax, credits, and payments	22	Enter the amount from line 21 (adjusted gross income).		22	
	23a	Check if: ☐ You were born before January 2, 1949, ☐ Blind ☐ Spouse was born before January 2, 1949, ☐ Blind, Total boxes checked ► 23a			
	b	If you are married filing separately and your spouse itemizes deductions, check here ► 23b ☐			
Standard Deduction for— • People who check any box on line 23a or 23b or who can be claimed as a dependent, see instructions. • All others: Single or Married filing separately, $6,100 Married filing jointly or Qualifying widow(er), $12,200 Head of household, $8,950	24	Enter your **standard deduction**.		24	
	25	Subtract line 24 from line 22. If line 24 is more than line 22, enter -0-.		25	
	26	**Exemptions.** Multiply $3,900 by the number on line 6d.		26	
	27	Subtract line 26 from line 25. If line 26 is more than line 25, enter -0-. This is your **taxable income**.	►	27	
	28	**Tax**, including any alternative minimum tax (see instructions).		28	
	29	Credit for child and dependent care expenses. Attach Form 2441.	29		
	30	Credit for the elderly or the disabled. Attach Schedule R.	30		
	31	Education credits from Form 8863, line 19.	31		
	32	Retirement savings contributions credit. Attach Form 8880.	32		
	33	Child tax credit. Attach Schedule 8812, if required.	33		
	34	Add lines 29 through 33. These are your **total credits**.		34	
	35	Subtract line 34 from line 28. If line 34 is more than line 28, enter -0-. This is your **total tax**.		35	
	36	Federal income tax withheld from Forms W-2 and 1099.	36		
If you have a qualifying child, attach Schedule EIC.	37	2013 estimated tax payments and amount applied from 2012 return.	37		
	38a	**Earned income credit (EIC)**.	38a		
	b	Nontaxable combat pay election.	38b		
	39	Additional child tax credit. Attach Schedule 8812.	39		
	40	American opportunity credit from Form 8863, line 8.	40		
	41	Add lines 36, 37, 38a, 39, and 40. These are your **total payments**.	►	41	
Refund	42	If line 41 is more than line 35, subtract line 35 from line 41. This is the amount you **overpaid**.		42	
Direct deposit? See instructions and fill in 43b, 43c, and 43d or Form 8888.	43a	Amount of line 42 you want **refunded to you**. If Form 8888 is attached, check here ► ☐ 43a			
	► b	Routing number [ ][ ][ ][ ][ ][ ][ ][ ][ ] ► c Type: ☐ Checking ☐ Savings			
	► d	Account number [ ][ ][ ][ ][ ][ ][ ][ ][ ][ ][ ][ ][ ][ ][ ][ ][ ]			
	44	Amount of line 42 you want **applied to your 2014 estimated tax**.	44		
Amount you owe	45	**Amount you owe.** Subtract line 41 from line 35. For details on how to pay, see instructions.	►	45	
	46	Estimated tax penalty (see instructions).	46		

Third party designee	Do you want to allow another person to discuss this return with the IRS (see instructions)? ☐ Yes. Complete the following. ☐ No		
	Designee's name ►	Phone no. ►	Personal identification number (PIN) ►

Sign here Joint return? See instructions. Keep a copy for your records.	Under penalties of perjury, I declare that I have examined this return and accompanying schedules and statements, and to the best of my knowledge and belief, they are true, correct, and accurately list all amounts and sources of income I received during the tax year. Declaration of preparer (other than the taxpayer) is based on all information of which the preparer has any knowledge.			
	Your signature	Date	Your occupation	Daytime phone number
	Spouse's signature. If a joint return, **both must sign**.	Date	Spouse's occupation	If the IRS sent you an Identity Protection PIN, enter it here (see inst.) [ ][ ][ ][ ][ ][ ]

Paid preparer use only	Print/type preparer's name	Preparer's signature		Date	Check ► ☐ if self-employed	PTIN
	Firm's name ►				Firm's EIN ►	
	Firm's address ►				Phone no.	

Form **1040A** (2013)

2013 Tax Table—Continued

If line 43 (taxable income) is—		And you are—			
At least	But less than	Single	Married filing jointly *	Married filing separately	Head of a household
		Your tax is—			
21,000					
21,000	21,050	2,708	2,261	2,708	2,516
21,050	21,100	2,715	2,269	2,715	2,524
21,100	21,150	2,723	2,276	2,723	2,531
21,150	21,200	2,730	2,284	2,730	2,539
21,200	21,250	2,738	2,291	2,738	2,546
21,250	21,300	2,745	2,299	2,745	2,554
21,300	21,350	2,753	2,306	2,753	2,561
21,350	21,400	2,760	2,314	2,760	2,569
21,400	21,450	2,768	2,321	2,768	2,576
21,450	21,500	2,775	2,329	2,775	2,584
21,500	21,550	2,783	2,336	2,783	2,591
21,550	21,600	2,790	2,344	2,790	2,599
21,600	21,650	2,798	2,351	2,798	2,606
21,650	21,700	2,805	2,359	2,805	2,614
21,700	21,750	2,813	2,366	2,813	2,621
21,750	21,800	2,820	2,374	2,820	2,629
21,800	21,850	2,828	2,381	2,828	2,636
21,850	21,900	2,835	2,389	2,835	2,644
21,900	21,950	2,843	2,396	2,843	2,651
21,950	22,000	2,850	2,404	2,850	2,659
22,000					
22,000	22,050	2,858	2,411	2,858	2,666
22,050	22,100	2,865	2,419	2,865	2,674
22,100	22,150	2,873	2,426	2,873	2,681
22,150	22,200	2,880	2,434	2,880	2,689
22,200	22,250	2,888	2,441	2,888	2,696
22,250	22,300	2,895	2,449	2,895	2,704
22,300	22,350	2,903	2,456	2,903	2,711
22,350	22,400	2,910	2,464	2,910	2,719
22,400	22,450	2,918	2,471	2,918	2,726
22,450	22,500	2,925	2,479	2,925	2,734
22,500	22,550	2,933	2,486	2,933	2,741
22,550	22,600	2,940	2,494	2,940	2,749
22,600	22,650	2,948	2,501	2,948	2,756
22,650	22,700	2,955	2,509	2,955	2,764
22,700	22,750	2,963	2,516	2,963	2,771
22,750	22,800	2,970	2,524	2,970	2,779
22,800	22,850	2,978	2,531	2,978	2,786
22,850	22,900	2,985	2,539	2,985	2,794
22,900	22,950	2,993	2,546	2,993	2,801
22,950	23,000	3,000	2,554	3,000	2,809
23,000					
23,000	23,050	3,008	2,561	3,008	2,816
23,050	23,100	3,015	2,569	3,015	2,824
23,100	23,150	3,023	2,576	3,023	2,831
23,150	23,200	3,030	2,584	3,030	2,839
23,200	23,250	3,038	2,591	3,038	2,846
23,250	23,300	3,045	2,599	3,045	2,854
23,300	23,350	3,053	2,606	3,053	2,861
23,350	23,400	3,060	2,614	3,060	2,869
23,400	23,450	3,068	2,621	3,068	2,876
23,450	23,500	3,075	2,629	3,075	2,884
23,500	23,550	3,083	2,636	3,083	2,891
23,550	23,600	3,090	2,644	3,090	2,899
23,600	23,650	3,098	2,651	3,098	2,906
23,650	23,700	3,105	2,659	3,105	2,914
23,700	23,750	3,113	2,666	3,113	2,921
23,750	23,800	3,120	2,674	3,120	2,929
23,800	23,850	3,128	2,681	3,128	2,936
23,850	23,900	3,135	2,689	3,135	2,944
23,900	23,950	3,143	2,696	3,143	2,951
23,950	24,000	3,150	2,704	3,150	2,959

If line 43 (taxable income) is—		And you are—			
At least	But less than	Single	Married filing jointly *	Married filing separately	Head of a household
		Your tax is—			
24,000					
24,000	24,050	3,158	2,711	3,158	2,966
24,050	24,100	3,165	2,719	3,165	2,974
24,100	24,150	3,173	2,726	3,173	2,981
24,150	24,200	3,180	2,734	3,180	2,989
24,200	24,250	3,188	2,741	3,188	2,996
24,250	24,300	3,195	2,749	3,195	3,004
24,300	24,350	3,203	2,756	3,203	3,011
24,350	24,400	3,210	2,764	3,210	3,019
24,400	24,450	3,218	2,771	3,218	3,026
24,450	24,500	3,225	2,779	3,225	3,034
24,500	24,550	3,233	2,786	3,233	3,041
24,550	24,600	3,240	2,794	3,240	3,049
24,600	24,650	3,248	2,801	3,248	3,056
24,650	24,700	3,255	2,809	3,255	3,064
24,700	24,750	3,263	2,816	3,263	3,071
24,750	24,800	3,270	2,824	3,270	3,079
24,800	24,850	3,278	2,831	3,278	3,086
24,850	24,900	3,285	2,839	3,285	3,094
24,900	24,950	3,293	2,846	3,293	3,101
24,950	25,000	3,300	2,854	3,300	3,109
25,000					
25,000	25,050	3,308	2,861	3,308	3,116
25,050	25,100	3,315	2,869	3,315	3,124
25,100	25,150	3,323	2,876	3,323	3,131
25,150	25,200	3,330	2,884	3,330	3,139
25,200	25,250	3,338	2,891	3,338	3,146
25,250	25,300	3,345	2,899	3,345	3,154
25,300	25,350	3,353	2,906	3,353	3,161
25,350	25,400	3,360	2,914	3,360	3,169
25,400	25,450	3,368	2,921	3,368	3,176
25,450	25,500	3,375	2,929	3,375	3,184
25,500	25,550	3,383	2,936	3,383	3,191
25,550	25,600	3,390	2,944	3,390	3,199
25,600	25,650	3,398	2,951	3,398	3,206
25,650	25,700	3,405	2,959	3,405	3,214
25,700	25,750	3,413	2,966	3,413	3,221
25,750	25,800	3,420	2,974	3,420	3,229
25,800	25,850	3,428	2,981	3,428	3,236
25,850	25,900	3,435	2,989	3,435	3,244
25,900	25,950	3,443	2,996	3,443	3,251
25,950	26,000	3,450	3,004	3,450	3,259
26,000					
26,000	26,050	3,458	3,011	3,458	3,266
26,050	26,100	3,465	3,019	3,465	3,274
26,100	26,150	3,473	3,026	3,473	3,281
26,150	26,200	3,480	3,034	3,480	3,289
26,200	26,250	3,488	3,041	3,488	3,296
26,250	26,300	3,495	3,049	3,495	3,304
26,300	26,350	3,503	3,056	3,503	3,311
26,350	26,400	3,510	3,064	3,510	3,319
26,400	26,450	3,518	3,071	3,518	3,326
26,450	26,500	3,525	3,079	3,525	3,334
26,500	26,550	3,533	3,086	3,533	3,341
26,550	26,600	3,540	3,094	3,540	3,349
26,600	26,650	3,548	3,101	3,548	3,356
26,650	26,700	3,555	3,109	3,555	3,364
26,700	26,750	3,563	3,116	3,563	3,371
26,750	26,800	3,570	3,124	3,570	3,379
26,800	26,850	3,578	3,131	3,578	3,386
26,850	26,900	3,585	3,139	3,585	3,394
26,900	26,950	3,593	3,146	3,593	3,401
26,950	27,000	3,600	3,154	3,600	3,409

If line 43 (taxable income) is—		And you are—			
At least	But less than	Single	Married filing jointly *	Married filing separately	Head of a household
		Your tax is—			
27,000					
27,000	27,050	3,608	3,161	3,608	3,416
27,050	27,100	3,615	3,169	3,615	3,424
27,100	27,150	3,623	3,176	3,623	3,431
27,150	27,200	3,630	3,184	3,630	3,439
27,200	27,250	3,638	3,191	3,638	3,446
27,250	27,300	3,645	3,199	3,645	3,454
27,300	27,350	3,653	3,206	3,653	3,461
27,350	27,400	3,660	3,214	3,660	3,469
27,400	27,450	3,668	3,221	3,668	3,476
27,450	27,500	3,675	3,229	3,675	3,484
27,500	27,550	3,683	3,236	3,683	3,491
27,550	27,600	3,690	3,244	3,690	3,499
27,600	27,650	3,698	3,251	3,698	3,506
27,650	27,700	3,705	3,259	3,705	3,514
27,700	27,750	3,713	3,266	3,713	3,521
27,750	27,800	3,720	3,274	3,720	3,529
27,800	27,850	3,728	3,281	3,728	3,536
27,850	27,900	3,735	3,289	3,735	3,544
27,900	27,950	3,743	3,296	3,743	3,551
27,950	28,000	3,750	3,304	3,750	3,559
28,000					
28,000	28,050	3,758	3,311	3,758	3,566
28,050	28,100	3,765	3,319	3,765	3,574
28,100	28,150	3,773	3,326	3,773	3,581
28,150	28,200	3,780	3,334	3,780	3,589
28,200	28,250	3,788	3,341	3,788	3,596
28,250	28,300	3,795	3,349	3,795	3,604
28,300	28,350	3,803	3,356	3,803	3,611
28,350	28,400	3,810	3,364	3,810	3,619
28,400	28,450	3,818	3,371	3,818	3,626
28,450	28,500	3,825	3,379	3,825	3,634
28,500	28,550	3,833	3,386	3,833	3,641
28,550	28,600	3,840	3,394	3,840	3,649
28,600	28,650	3,848	3,401	3,848	3,656
28,650	28,700	3,855	3,409	3,855	3,664
28,700	28,750	3,863	3,416	3,863	3,671
28,750	28,800	3,870	3,424	3,870	3,679
28,800	28,850	3,878	3,431	3,878	3,686
28,850	28,900	3,885	3,439	3,885	3,694
28,900	28,950	3,893	3,446	3,893	3,701
28,950	29,000	3,900	3,454	3,900	3,709
29,000					
29,000	29,050	3,908	3,461	3,908	3,716
29,050	29,100	3,915	3,469	3,915	3,724
29,100	29,150	3,923	3,476	3,923	3,731
29,150	29,200	3,930	3,484	3,930	3,739
29,200	29,250	3,938	3,491	3,938	3,746
29,250	29,300	3,945	3,499	3,945	3,754
29,300	29,350	3,953	3,506	3,953	3,761
29,350	29,400	3,960	3,514	3,960	3,769
29,400	29,450	3,968	3,521	3,968	3,776
29,450	29,500	3,975	3,529	3,975	3,784
29,500	29,550	3,983	3,536	3,983	3,791
29,550	29,600	3,990	3,544	3,990	3,799
29,600	29,650	3,998	3,551	3,998	3,806
29,650	29,700	4,005	3,559	4,005	3,814
29,700	29,750	4,013	3,566	4,013	3,821
29,750	29,800	4,020	3,574	4,020	3,829
29,800	29,850	4,028	3,581	4,028	3,836
29,850	29,900	4,035	3,589	4,035	3,844
29,900	29,950	4,043	3,596	4,043	3,851
29,950	30,000	4,050	3,604	4,050	3,859

(Continued)

* This column must also be used by a qualifying widow(er).

2013 Tax Table—Continued

If line 43 (taxable income) is— At least	But less than	And you are— Single	Married filing jointly *	Married filing separately	Head of a household
30,000					
30,000	30,050	4,058	3,611	4,058	3,866
30,050	30,100	4,065	3,619	4,065	3,874
30,100	30,150	4,073	3,626	4,073	3,881
30,150	30,200	4,080	3,634	4,080	3,889
30,200	30,250	4,088	3,641	4,088	3,896
30,250	30,300	4,095	3,649	4,095	3,904
30,300	30,350	4,103	3,656	4,103	3,911
30,350	30,400	4,110	3,664	4,110	3,919
30,400	30,450	4,118	3,671	4,118	3,926
30,450	30,500	4,125	3,679	4,125	3,934
30,500	30,550	4,133	3,686	4,133	3,941
30,550	30,600	4,140	3,694	4,140	3,949
30,600	30,650	4,148	3,701	4,148	3,956
30,650	30,700	4,155	3,709	4,155	3,964
30,700	30,750	4,163	3,716	4,163	3,971
30,750	30,800	4,170	3,724	4,170	3,979
30,800	30,850	4,178	3,731	4,178	3,986
30,850	30,900	4,185	3,739	4,185	3,994
30,900	30,950	4,193	3,746	4,193	4,001
30,950	31,000	4,200	3,754	4,200	4,009
31,000					
31,000	31,050	4,208	3,761	4,208	4,016
31,050	31,100	4,215	3,769	4,215	4,024
31,100	31,150	4,223	3,776	4,223	4,031
31,150	31,200	4,230	3,784	4,230	4,039
31,200	31,250	4,238	3,791	4,238	4,046
31,250	31,300	4,245	3,799	4,245	4,054
31,300	31,350	4,253	3,806	4,253	4,061
31,350	31,400	4,260	3,814	4,260	4,069
31,400	31,450	4,268	3,821	4,268	4,076
31,450	31,500	4,275	3,829	4,275	4,084
31,500	31,550	4,283	3,836	4,283	4,091
31,550	31,600	4,290	3,844	4,290	4,099
31,600	31,650	4,298	3,851	4,298	4,106
31,650	31,700	4,305	3,859	4,305	4,114
31,700	31,750	4,313	3,866	4,313	4,121
31,750	31,800	4,320	3,874	4,320	4,129
31,800	31,850	4,328	3,881	4,328	4,136
31,850	31,900	4,335	3,889	4,335	4,144
31,900	31,950	4,343	3,896	4,343	4,151
31,950	32,000	4,350	3,904	4,350	4,159
32,000					
32,000	32,050	4,358	3,911	4,358	4,166
32,050	32,100	4,365	3,919	4,365	4,174
32,100	32,150	4,373	3,926	4,373	4,181
32,150	32,200	4,380	3,934	4,380	4,189
32,200	32,250	4,388	3,941	4,388	4,196
32,250	32,300	4,395	3,949	4,395	4,204
32,300	32,350	4,403	3,956	4,403	4,211
32,350	32,400	4,410	3,964	4,410	4,219
32,400	32,450	4,418	3,971	4,418	4,226
32,450	32,500	4,425	3,979	4,425	4,234
32,500	32,550	4,433	3,986	4,433	4,241
32,550	32,600	4,440	3,994	4,440	4,249
32,600	32,650	4,448	4,001	4,448	4,256
32,650	32,700	4,455	4,009	4,455	4,264
32,700	32,750	4,463	4,016	4,463	4,271
32,750	32,800	4,470	4,024	4,470	4,279
32,800	32,850	4,478	4,031	4,478	4,286
32,850	32,900	4,485	4,039	4,485	4,294
32,900	32,950	4,493	4,046	4,493	4,301
32,950	33,000	4,500	4,054	4,500	4,309

If line 43 (taxable income) is— At least	But less than	And you are— Single	Married filing jointly *	Married filing separately	Head of a household
33,000					
33,000	33,050	4,508	4,061	4,508	4,316
33,050	33,100	4,515	4,069	4,515	4,324
33,100	33,150	4,523	4,076	4,523	4,331
33,150	33,200	4,530	4,084	4,530	4,339
33,200	33,250	4,538	4,091	4,538	4,346
33,250	33,300	4,545	4,099	4,545	4,354
33,300	33,350	4,553	4,106	4,553	4,361
33,350	33,400	4,560	4,114	4,560	4,369
33,400	33,450	4,568	4,121	4,568	4,376
33,450	33,500	4,575	4,129	4,575	4,384
33,500	33,550	4,583	4,136	4,583	4,391
33,550	33,600	4,590	4,144	4,590	4,399
33,600	33,650	4,598	4,151	4,598	4,406
33,650	33,700	4,605	4,159	4,605	4,414
33,700	33,750	4,613	4,166	4,613	4,421
33,750	33,800	4,620	4,174	4,620	4,429
33,800	33,850	4,628	4,181	4,628	4,436
33,850	33,900	4,635	4,189	4,635	4,444
33,900	33,950	4,643	4,196	4,643	4,451
33,950	34,000	4,650	4,204	4,650	4,459
34,000					
34,000	34,050	4,658	4,211	4,658	4,466
34,050	34,100	4,665	4,219	4,665	4,474
34,100	34,150	4,673	4,226	4,673	4,481
34,150	34,200	4,680	4,234	4,680	4,489
34,200	34,250	4,688	4,241	4,688	4,496
34,250	34,300	4,695	4,249	4,695	4,504
34,300	34,350	4,703	4,256	4,703	4,511
34,350	34,400	4,710	4,264	4,710	4,519
34,400	34,450	4,718	4,271	4,718	4,526
34,450	34,500	4,725	4,279	4,725	4,534
34,500	34,550	4,733	4,286	4,733	4,541
34,550	34,600	4,740	4,294	4,740	4,549
34,600	34,650	4,748	4,301	4,748	4,556
34,650	34,700	4,755	4,309	4,755	4,564
34,700	34,750	4,763	4,316	4,763	4,571
34,750	34,800	4,770	4,324	4,770	4,579
34,800	34,850	4,778	4,331	4,778	4,586
34,850	34,900	4,785	4,339	4,785	4,594
34,900	34,950	4,793	4,346	4,793	4,601
34,950	35,000	4,800	4,354	4,800	4,609
35,000					
35,000	35,050	4,808	4,361	4,808	4,616
35,050	35,100	4,815	4,369	4,815	4,624
35,100	35,150	4,823	4,376	4,823	4,631
35,150	35,200	4,830	4,384	4,830	4,639
35,200	35,250	4,838	4,391	4,838	4,646
35,250	35,300	4,845	4,399	4,845	4,654
35,300	35,350	4,853	4,406	4,853	4,661
35,350	35,400	4,860	4,414	4,860	4,669
35,400	35,450	4,868	4,421	4,868	4,676
35,450	35,500	4,875	4,429	4,875	4,684
35,500	35,550	4,883	4,436	4,883	4,691
35,550	35,600	4,890	4,444	4,890	4,699
35,600	35,650	4,898	4,451	4,898	4,706
35,650	35,700	4,905	4,459	4,905	4,714
35,700	35,750	4,913	4,466	4,913	4,721
35,750	35,800	4,920	4,474	4,920	4,729
35,800	35,850	4,928	4,481	4,928	4,736
35,850	35,900	4,935	4,489	4,935	4,744
35,900	35,950	4,943	4,496	4,943	4,751
35,950	36,000	4,950	4,504	4,950	4,759

If line 43 (taxable income) is— At least	But less than	And you are— Single	Married filing jointly *	Married filing separately	Head of a household
36,000					
36,000	36,050	4,958	4,511	4,958	4,766
36,050	36,100	4,965	4,519	4,965	4,774
36,100	36,150	4,973	4,526	4,973	4,781
36,150	36,200	4,980	4,534	4,980	4,789
36,200	36,250	4,988	4,541	4,988	4,796
36,250	36,300	4,998	4,549	4,998	4,804
36,300	36,350	5,010	4,556	5,010	4,811
36,350	36,400	5,023	4,564	5,023	4,819
36,400	36,450	5,035	4,571	5,035	4,826
36,450	36,500	5,048	4,579	5,048	4,834
36,500	36,550	5,060	4,586	5,060	4,841
36,550	36,600	5,073	4,594	5,073	4,849
36,600	36,650	5,085	4,601	5,085	4,856
36,650	36,700	5,098	4,609	5,098	4,864
36,700	36,750	5,110	4,616	5,110	4,871
36,750	36,800	5,123	4,624	5,123	4,879
36,800	36,850	5,135	4,631	5,135	4,886
36,850	36,900	5,148	4,639	5,148	4,894
36,900	36,950	5,160	4,646	5,160	4,901
36,950	37,000	5,173	4,654	5,173	4,909
37,000					
37,000	37,050	5,185	4,661	5,185	4,916
37,050	37,100	5,198	4,669	5,198	4,924
37,100	37,150	5,210	4,676	5,210	4,931
37,150	37,200	5,223	4,684	5,223	4,939
37,200	37,250	5,235	4,691	5,235	4,946
37,250	37,300	5,248	4,699	5,248	4,954
37,300	37,350	5,260	4,706	5,260	4,961
37,350	37,400	5,273	4,714	5,273	4,969
37,400	37,450	5,285	4,721	5,285	4,976
37,450	37,500	5,298	4,729	5,298	4,984
37,500	37,550	5,310	4,736	5,310	4,991
37,550	37,600	5,323	4,744	5,323	4,999
37,600	37,650	5,335	4,751	5,335	5,006
37,650	37,700	5,348	4,759	5,348	5,014
37,700	37,750	5,360	4,766	5,360	5,021
37,750	37,800	5,373	4,774	5,373	5,029
37,800	37,850	5,385	4,781	5,385	5,036
37,850	37,900	5,398	4,789	5,398	5,044
37,900	37,950	5,410	4,796	5,410	5,051
37,950	38,000	5,423	4,804	5,423	5,059
38,000					
38,000	38,050	5,435	4,811	5,435	5,066
38,050	38,100	5,448	4,819	5,448	5,074
38,100	38,150	5,460	4,826	5,460	5,081
38,150	38,200	5,473	4,834	5,473	5,089
38,200	38,250	5,485	4,841	5,485	5,096
38,250	38,300	5,498	4,849	5,498	5,104
38,300	38,350	5,510	4,856	5,510	5,111
38,350	38,400	5,523	4,864	5,523	5,119
38,400	38,450	5,535	4,871	5,535	5,126
38,450	38,500	5,548	4,879	5,548	5,134
38,500	38,550	5,560	4,886	5,560	5,141
38,550	38,600	5,573	4,894	5,573	5,149
38,600	38,650	5,585	4,901	5,585	5,156
38,650	38,700	5,598	4,909	5,598	5,164
38,700	38,750	5,610	4,916	5,610	5,171
38,750	38,800	5,623	4,924	5,623	5,179
38,800	38,850	5,635	4,931	5,635	5,186
38,850	38,900	5,648	4,939	5,648	5,194
38,900	38,950	5,660	4,946	5,660	5,201
38,950	39,000	5,673	4,954	5,673	5,209

(Continued)

* This column must also be used by a qualifying widow(er).

2013 Tax Table—*Continued*

39,000 / 40,000 / 41,000

If line 43 (taxable income) is— At least	But less than	Single	Married filing jointly *	Married filing separately	Head of a household
39,000					
39,000	39,050	5,685	4,961	5,685	5,216
39,050	39,100	5,698	4,969	5,698	5,224
39,100	39,150	5,710	4,976	5,710	5,231
39,150	39,200	5,723	4,984	5,723	5,239
39,200	39,250	5,735	4,991	5,735	5,246
39,250	39,300	5,748	4,999	5,748	5,254
39,300	39,350	5,760	5,006	5,760	5,261
39,350	39,400	5,773	5,014	5,773	5,269
39,400	39,450	5,785	5,021	5,785	5,276
39,450	39,500	5,798	5,029	5,798	5,284
39,500	39,550	5,810	5,036	5,810	5,291
39,550	39,600	5,823	5,044	5,823	5,299
39,600	39,650	5,835	5,051	5,835	5,306
39,650	39,700	5,848	5,059	5,848	5,314
39,700	39,750	5,860	5,066	5,860	5,321
39,750	39,800	5,873	5,074	5,873	5,329
39,800	39,850	5,885	5,081	5,885	5,336
39,850	39,900	5,898	5,089	5,898	5,344
39,900	39,950	5,910	5,096	5,910	5,351
39,950	40,000	5,923	5,104	5,923	5,359
40,000					
40,000	40,050	5,935	5,111	5,935	5,366
40,050	40,100	5,948	5,119	5,948	5,374
40,100	40,150	5,960	5,126	5,960	5,381
40,150	40,200	5,973	5,134	5,973	5,389
40,200	40,250	5,985	5,141	5,985	5,396
40,250	40,300	5,998	5,149	5,998	5,404
40,300	40,350	6,010	5,156	6,010	5,411
40,350	40,400	6,023	5,164	6,023	5,419
40,400	40,450	6,035	5,171	6,035	5,426
40,450	40,500	6,048	5,179	6,048	5,434
40,500	40,550	6,060	5,186	6,060	5,441
40,550	40,600	6,073	5,194	6,073	5,449
40,600	40,650	6,085	5,201	6,085	5,456
40,650	40,700	6,098	5,209	6,098	5,464
40,700	40,750	6,110	5,216	6,110	5,471
40,750	40,800	6,123	5,224	6,123	5,479
40,800	40,850	6,135	5,231	6,135	5,486
40,850	40,900	6,148	5,239	6,148	5,494
40,900	40,950	6,160	5,246	6,160	5,501
40,950	41,000	6,173	5,254	6,173	5,509
41,000					
41,000	41,050	6,185	5,261	6,185	5,516
41,050	41,100	6,198	5,269	6,198	5,524
41,100	41,150	6,210	5,276	6,210	5,531
41,150	41,200	6,223	5,284	6,223	5,539
41,200	41,250	6,235	5,291	6,235	5,546
41,250	41,300	6,248	5,299	6,248	5,554
41,300	41,350	6,260	5,306	6,260	5,561
41,350	41,400	6,273	5,314	6,273	5,569
41,400	41,450	6,285	5,321	6,285	5,576
41,450	41,500	6,298	5,329	6,298	5,584
41,500	41,550	6,310	5,336	6,310	5,591
41,550	41,600	6,323	5,344	6,323	5,599
41,600	41,650	6,335	5,351	6,335	5,606
41,650	41,700	6,348	5,359	6,348	5,614
41,700	41,750	6,360	5,366	6,360	5,621
41,750	41,800	6,373	5,374	6,373	5,629
41,800	41,850	6,385	5,381	6,385	5,636
41,850	41,900	6,398	5,389	6,398	5,644
41,900	41,950	6,410	5,396	6,410	5,651
41,950	42,000	6,423	5,404	6,423	5,659

42,000 / 43,000 / 44,000

If line 43 (taxable income) is— At least	But less than	Single	Married filing jointly *	Married filing separately	Head of a household
42,000					
42,000	42,050	6,435	5,411	6,435	5,666
42,050	42,100	6,448	5,419	6,448	5,674
42,100	42,150	6,460	5,426	6,460	5,681
42,150	42,200	6,473	5,434	6,473	5,689
42,200	42,250	6,485	5,441	6,485	5,696
42,250	42,300	6,498	5,449	6,498	5,704
42,300	42,350	6,510	5,456	6,510	5,711
42,350	42,400	6,523	5,464	6,523	5,719
42,400	42,450	6,535	5,471	6,535	5,726
42,450	42,500	6,548	5,479	6,548	5,734
42,500	42,550	6,560	5,486	6,560	5,741
42,550	42,600	6,573	5,494	6,573	5,749
42,600	42,650	6,585	5,501	6,585	5,756
42,650	42,700	6,598	5,509	6,598	5,764
42,700	42,750	6,610	5,516	6,610	5,771
42,750	42,800	6,623	5,524	6,623	5,779
42,800	42,850	6,635	5,531	6,635	5,786
42,850	42,900	6,648	5,539	6,648	5,794
42,900	42,950	6,660	5,546	6,660	5,801
42,950	43,000	6,673	5,554	6,673	5,809
43,000					
43,000	43,050	6,685	5,561	6,685	5,816
43,050	43,100	6,698	5,569	6,698	5,824
43,100	43,150	6,710	5,576	6,710	5,831
43,150	43,200	6,723	5,584	6,723	5,839
43,200	43,250	6,735	5,591	6,735	5,846
43,250	43,300	6,748	5,599	6,748	5,854
43,300	43,350	6,760	5,606	6,760	5,861
43,350	43,400	6,773	5,614	6,773	5,869
43,400	43,450	6,785	5,621	6,785	5,876
43,450	43,500	6,798	5,629	6,798	5,884
43,500	43,550	6,810	5,636	6,810	5,891
43,550	43,600	6,823	5,644	6,823	5,899
43,600	43,650	6,835	5,651	6,835	5,906
43,650	43,700	6,848	5,659	6,848	5,914
43,700	43,750	6,860	5,666	6,860	5,921
43,750	43,800	6,873	5,674	6,873	5,929
43,800	43,850	6,885	5,681	6,885	5,936
43,850	43,900	6,898	5,689	6,898	5,944
43,900	43,950	6,910	5,696	6,910	5,951
43,950	44,000	6,923	5,704	6,923	5,959
44,000					
44,000	44,050	6,935	5,711	6,935	5,966
44,050	44,100	6,948	5,719	6,948	5,974
44,100	44,150	6,960	5,726	6,960	5,981
44,150	44,200	6,973	5,734	6,973	5,989
44,200	44,250	6,985	5,741	6,985	5,996
44,250	44,300	6,998	5,749	6,998	6,004
44,300	44,350	7,010	5,756	7,010	6,011
44,350	44,400	7,023	5,764	7,023	6,019
44,400	44,450	7,035	5,771	7,035	6,026
44,450	44,500	7,048	5,779	7,048	6,034
44,500	44,550	7,060	5,786	7,060	6,041
44,550	44,600	7,073	5,794	7,073	6,049
44,600	44,650	7,085	5,801	7,085	6,056
44,650	44,700	7,098	5,809	7,098	6,064
44,700	44,750	7,110	5,816	7,110	6,071
44,750	44,800	7,123	5,824	7,123	6,079
44,800	44,850	7,135	5,831	7,135	6,086
44,850	44,900	7,148	5,839	7,148	6,094
44,900	44,950	7,160	5,846	7,160	6,101
44,950	45,000	7,173	5,854	7,173	6,109

45,000 / 46,000 / 47,000

If line 43 (taxable income) is— At least	But less than	Single	Married filing jointly *	Married filing separately	Head of a household
45,000					
45,000	45,050	7,185	5,861	7,185	6,116
45,050	45,100	7,198	5,869	7,198	6,124
45,100	45,150	7,210	5,876	7,210	6,131
45,150	45,200	7,223	5,884	7,223	6,139
45,200	45,250	7,235	5,891	7,235	6,146
45,250	45,300	7,248	5,899	7,248	6,154
45,300	45,350	7,260	5,906	7,260	6,161
45,350	45,400	7,273	5,914	7,273	6,169
45,400	45,450	7,285	5,921	7,285	6,176
45,450	45,500	7,298	5,929	7,298	6,184
45,500	45,550	7,310	5,936	7,310	6,191
45,550	45,600	7,323	5,944	7,323	6,199
45,600	45,650	7,335	5,951	7,335	6,206
45,650	45,700	7,348	5,959	7,348	6,214
45,700	45,750	7,360	5,966	7,360	6,221
45,750	45,800	7,373	5,974	7,373	6,229
45,800	45,850	7,385	5,981	7,385	6,236
45,850	45,900	7,398	5,989	7,398	6,244
45,900	45,950	7,410	5,996	7,410	6,251
45,950	46,000	7,423	6,004	7,423	6,259
46,000					
46,000	46,050	7,435	6,011	7,435	6,266
46,050	46,100	7,448	6,019	7,448	6,274
46,100	46,150	7,460	6,026	7,460	6,281
46,150	46,200	7,473	6,034	7,473	6,289
46,200	46,250	7,485	6,041	7,485	6,296
46,250	46,300	7,498	6,049	7,498	6,304
46,300	46,350	7,510	6,056	7,510	6,311
46,350	46,400	7,523	6,064	7,523	6,319
46,400	46,450	7,535	6,071	7,535	6,326
46,450	46,500	7,548	6,079	7,548	6,334
46,500	46,550	7,560	6,086	7,560	6,341
46,550	46,600	7,573	6,094	7,573	6,349
46,600	46,650	7,585	6,101	7,585	6,356
46,650	46,700	7,598	6,109	7,598	6,364
46,700	46,750	7,610	6,116	7,610	6,371
46,750	46,800	7,623	6,124	7,623	6,379
46,800	46,850	7,635	6,131	7,635	6,386
46,850	46,900	7,648	6,139	7,648	6,394
46,900	46,950	7,660	6,146	7,660	6,401
46,950	47,000	7,673	6,154	7,673	6,409
47,000					
47,000	47,050	7,685	6,161	7,685	6,416
47,050	47,100	7,698	6,169	7,698	6,424
47,100	47,150	7,710	6,176	7,710	6,431
47,150	47,200	7,723	6,184	7,723	6,439
47,200	47,250	7,735	6,191	7,735	6,446
47,250	47,300	7,748	6,199	7,748	6,454
47,300	47,350	7,760	6,206	7,760	6,461
47,350	47,400	7,773	6,214	7,773	6,469
47,400	47,450	7,785	6,221	7,785	6,476
47,450	47,500	7,798	6,229	7,798	6,484
47,500	47,550	7,810	6,236	7,810	6,491
47,550	47,600	7,823	6,244	7,823	6,499
47,600	47,650	7,835	6,251	7,835	6,506
47,650	47,700	7,848	6,259	7,848	6,514
47,700	47,750	7,860	6,266	7,860	6,521
47,750	47,800	7,873	6,274	7,873	6,529
47,800	47,850	7,885	6,281	7,885	6,536
47,850	47,900	7,898	6,289	7,898	6,544
47,900	47,950	7,910	6,296	7,910	6,551
47,950	48,000	7,923	6,304	7,923	6,559

(Continued)

* This column must also be used by a qualifying widow(er).

Create a new budget for Mary to help her get organized. What advice would you give Mary to get out of debt, increase her credit score, save for emergencies, save for retirement, and meet her goals of owning a car and home?

CATEGORY	Monthly Amount	New Monthly Budget	Comment
Income:			
Wages and Bonuses	$4,000		
Interest Income	$1		
Investment Income	0		
Other Income	0		
Income Subtotal	$4,001		
Less Income Tax Withheld:			
Federal Income Tax	$375		
State and Local Tax	$233		
Social Security and Medicare tax	$306		
Income Taxes Subtotal	$914		
Net Income	$3,087		
Expenses			
Rent	$850		
Health Insurance	$308		
Savings	$100		
Utilities	$274		Includes electric, gas, water, cable, and internet expenses
Greg's Installment ($1,200)	$100		
Mable's ($1,900)	$125		
Dante's ($1,000)	$100		
MasterCard ($900)	$40		
Student Loan	$200		
Transportation	$105		

Food	$315		
Salon	$150		
Retirement Plan	0		
Miscellaneous	0		
Less Total Expenses	$2,667		
Total Disposable Income	$420		

Appendix I

Solution: Tax Preparation

Form **1040A**	Department of the Treasury—Internal Revenue Service **U.S. Individual Income Tax Return** (99)	**2013**	IRS Use Only—Do not write or staple in this space.

Your first name and initial	Last name		OMB No. 1545-0074
Mary	Bell		**Your social security number** 123 45 6789
If a joint return, spouse's first name and initial	Last name		**Spouse's social security number**

Home address (number and street). If you have a P.O. box, see instructions.	Apt. no.	▲ Make sure the SSN(s) above
3620 Beaver Street	3-B	and on line 6c are correct.

City, town or post office, state, and ZIP code. If you have a foreign address, also complete spaces below (see instructions).
Atlanta GA 30013

Foreign country name	Foreign province/state/county	Foreign postal code

Presidential Election Campaign
Check here if you, or your spouse if filing jointly, want $3 to go to this fund. Checking a box below will not change your tax or refund. ☐ You ☐ Spouse

Filing status
Check only one box.

1 ☒ Single
2 ☐ Married filing jointly (even if only one had income)
3 ☐ Married filing separately. Enter spouse's SSN above and full name here. ▶
4 ☐ Head of household (with qualifying person). (See instructions.) If the qualifying person is a child but not your dependent, enter this child's name here. ▶
5 ☐ Qualifying widow(er) with dependent child (see instructions)

Exemptions

6a ☒ Yourself. If someone can claim you as a dependent, **do not check** box 6a.
b ☐ Spouse

c Dependents:

If more than six dependents, see instructions.

(1) First name Last name	(2) Dependent's social security number	(3) Dependent's relationship to you	(4) ✓ if child under age 17 qualifying for child tax credit (see instructions)
			☐
			☐
			☐
			☐
			☐
			☐

Boxes checked on 6a and 6b **1**
No. of children on 6c who:
• lived with you
• did not live with you due to divorce or separation (see instructions)
Dependents on 6c not entered above
Add numbers on lines above ▶ **1**

d Total number of exemptions claimed.

Income

Attach Form(s) W-2 here. Also attach Form(s) 1099-R if tax was withheld.

If you did not get a W-2, see instructions.

7	Wages, salaries, tips, etc. Attach Form(s) W-2.	7	48,000.
8a	**Taxable interest. Attach Schedule B if required.**	8a	12.
b	Tax-exempt interest. **Do not include on line 8a.** 8b		
9a	Ordinary dividends. Attach Schedule B if required.	9a	
b	Qualified dividends (see instructions). 9b		
10	Capital gain distributions (see instructions).	10	
11a	IRA distributions. 11a	11b Taxable amount (see instructions). 11b	
12a	Pensions and annuities. 12a	12b Taxable amount (see instructions). 12b	
13	Unemployment compensation and Alaska Permanent Fund dividends.	13	
14a	Social security benefits. 14a	14b Taxable amount (see instructions). 14b	
15	Add lines 7 through 14b (far right column). This is your **total income.** ▶	15	48,012.

Adjusted gross income

16	Educator expenses (see instructions).	16	
17	IRA deduction (see instructions).	17	
18	Student loan interest deduction (see instructions).	18 485.	
19	Tuition and fees. Attach Form 8917.	19	
20	Add lines 16 through 19. These are your **total adjustments.**	20	485.
21	Subtract line 20 from line 15. This is your **adjusted gross income.** ▶	21	47,527.

For Disclosure, Privacy Act, and Paperwork Reduction Act Notice, see separate instructions. BAA

Form **1040A** (2013)

REV 03/03/14 TTW

Form 1040A (2013)   Page **2**

Tax, credits, and payments	22	Enter the amount from line 21 (adjusted gross income).		22	47,527.
	23a	Check { You were born before January 2, 1949, ☐ Blind } Total boxes			
		If: { Spouse was born before January 2, 1949, ☐ Blind } checked ▶ 23a	☐		
	b	If you are married filing separately and your spouse itemizes deductions, check here ▶ 23b	☐		
Standard Deduction for—	24	Enter your **standard deduction.**		24	6,100.
• People who check any box on line 23a or 23b or who can be claimed as a dependent, see instructions.	25	Subtract line 24 from line 22. If line 24 is more than line 22, enter -0-.		25	41,427.
	26	**Exemptions.** Multiply $3,900 by the number on line 6d.		26	3,900.
	27	Subtract line 26 from line 25. If line 26 is more than line 25, enter -0-. This is your **taxable income.**	▶	27	37,527.
• All others: Single or Married filing separately, $6,100	28	**Tax,** including any alternative minimum tax (see instructions).		28	5,310.
	29	Credit for child and dependent care expenses. Attach Form 2441.	29		
Married filing jointly or Qualifying widow(er), $12,200	30	Credit for the elderly or the disabled. Attach Schedule R.	30		
	31	Education credits from Form 8863, line 19.	31		
Head of household, $8,950	32	Retirement savings contributions credit. Attach Form 8880.	32		
	33	Child tax credit. Attach Schedule 8812, if required.	33		
	34	Add lines 29 through 33. These are your **total credits.**		34	
	35	Subtract line 34 from line 28. If line 34 is more than line 28, enter -0-. This is your **total tax.**		35	5,310.
	36	Federal income tax withheld from Forms W-2 and 1099.	36	4,500.	
If you have a qualifying child, attach Schedule EIC.	37	2013 estimated tax payments and amount applied from 2012 return.	37		
	38a	**Earned income credit (EIC).**	38a		
	b	Nontaxable combat pay election. 38b			
	39	Additional child tax credit. Attach Schedule 8812.	39		
	40	American opportunity credit from Form 8863, line 8.	40		
	41	Add lines 36, 37, 38a, 39, and 40. These are your **total payments.** ▶		41	4,500.
Refund	42	If line 41 is more than line 35, subtract line 35 from line 41. This is the amount you **overpaid.**		42	
Direct deposit? See instructions and fill in 43b, 43c, and 43d or Form 8888.	43a	Amount of line 42 you want **refunded to you.** If Form 8888 is attached, check here ▶ 43a		☐	
	▶ b	Routing number XXXXXXXXX ▶ c Type: ☐ Checking ☐ Savings			
	▶ d	Account number XXXXXXXXXXXXXXXXX			
	44	Amount of line 42 you want **applied to your 2014 estimated tax.**	44		
Amount you owe	45	**Amount you owe.** Subtract line 41 from line 35. For details on how to pay, see instructions. ▶		45	810.
	46	Estimated tax penalty (see instructions).	46		

Third party designee — Do you want to allow another person to discuss this return with the IRS (see instructions)? ☐ **Yes.** Complete the following. ☒ **No**

Designee's name   Phone no. ▶   Personal identification number (PIN) ▶

Sign here — Under penalties of perjury, I declare that I have examined this return and accompanying schedules and statements, and to the best of my knowledge and belief, they are true, correct, and accurately list all amounts and sources of income I received during the tax year. Declaration of preparer (other than the taxpayer) is based on all information of which the preparer has any knowledge.

Joint return? See instructions. Keep a copy for your records.

Your signature *Mary Bell*   Date 2/1/2014   Your occupation Accountant   Daytime phone number

Spouse's signature. If a joint return, **both must sign.**   Date   Spouse's occupation   If the IRS sent you an Identity Protection PIN, enter it here (see inst.)

Paid preparer use only

Print/type preparer's name   Preparer's signature   Date   Check ▶ ☐ if self-employed   PTIN

Firm's name ▶ Self-Prepared   Firm's EIN ▶

Firm's address ▶   Phone no.

REV 03/03/14 TTW   Form **1040A** (2013)

Appendix II

Solution: New Budget

CATEGORY	Monthly Amount	New Monthly Budget	Comment
Income:			
Wages and Bonuses	$4,000	$4,000	
Interest Income	$1	$1	
Investment Income	0	0	
Other Income	0	0	
Income Subtotal	$4,001	$4,001	
Less Income Tax Withheld:			
Federal Income Tax	$375	$445	Increase withholding to avoid an estimated tax penalty
State and Local Tax	$233	$233	
Social Security and Medicare tax	$306	$306	
Income Taxes Subtotal	$914	$984	
Net Income	$3,087	$3,017	
Expenses			
Rent	$850	$850	
Health Insurance	$308	$308	
Savings	$100	$150	Increase savings for emergencies and goals
Utilities	$274	$274	Includes: electric, gas, water, cable, and internet expenses
Greg's Installment ($1,200)	$100	$100	
Mable's ($1,900)	$125	$125	

Dante's ($1,000)	$100	$200	Increase payment to retire this debt
MasterCard ($900)	$40	$40	
Student Loan	$200	$200	
Transportation	$105	$105	
Food	$315	$315	
Salon	$150	$150	
Retirement Plan	0	$100	Start early contributing toward retirement
Miscellaneous	0	$100	Coffee, entertainment, etc.
Less Total Expenses	$2,667	$3017	
Total Disposable Income	$420	0	

Appendix III

Solution: Financial Advice

- Mary owes additional income tax of $810 for tax year 2013; she should withdraw funds from her savings account to cover her liability and avoid IRS interest and penalties. Mary is advised to increase her withholding in the year 2014 by $70 each month. The extra payments will ensure that Mary pays 100 percent of her prior year tax of $5,310 avoiding an estimated tax penalty.

- Currently, she is unable to buy a car and afford the cost to own it, until she reduces debt, save for emergencies and contribute to her retirement plan.

- Mary can increase her credit score and get out of debt by following a plan. Fortunately for Mary, she has disposable income she can use to reduce her debt. Allocate an additional $100 toward the debt to Dante's for a total of $200; she can retire the debt within five months. After Dante's is paid in full use the $200 plus the original $40 toward the Master Card balance of $900, to full pay within four months. Mary should continue the same strategy with Mable's and Greg's. Reducing debt improves credit scores.

- Mary should continue the same payment toward her student loan. The interest rate is low and the interest payments are tax deductible. In addition, student loan debt doesn't carry the same negative effect as revolving credit.

- Increase savings from $100 to $150 for emergencies, and meeting the goals of owning a car and a home. Have this amount automatically allocated from payroll. Increase savings allocations when debts are paid in full and income increases.

- Contribute $100 a month to the company's retirement plan; her employer will match dollar for dollar the first 5 percent of gross income. A contribution of $1,200 a year becomes $2,400. Contributions should increase in tandem with salary increases until the 8 percent match is achieved. Additional contributions can be made to a Roth IRA.

- Mary should only charge expenses for emergencies. As income increases, and debts are paid in full, Mary can allocate more toward miscellaneous cash expenditures to avoid charge card expenses.

- Once Mary is able to manage her recurring obligations, save for emergencies, and contribute to her retirement plan, she is ready to invest using discretionary income.

ABOUT THE AUTHOR

Merlon Harper is a freelance writer and holds an MBA degree in finance from Mercer University and a bachelor's degree in business administration from Alcorn State University. She has over thirty years of business and finance experience and volunteers at high schools teaching students financial literacy. She is passionate about personal finance and believes that every American should have the basic knowledge and skills to pursue his or her American dream. Merlon and her husband, Joseph, have two children and live in Covington, Georgia.

REFERENCES

"9 Fast Fixes for Repairing Your Credit." *CREDITSENSE* (blog). Accessed June 4, 2015. http://www.creditsense.com/blog/9-fast-fixes-for-repairing-your-credit/.

"9 Fixes To Your Credit Score." *CREDITSENSE* (blog). Accessed June 4, 2015. http://www.creditsense.com/blog/9-fixes-to-your-credit-score/.

Mangla, Ismat Sarah."Quest for the Perfect Credit Score". *The Credit Clinic (PDF)*. August 31, 2010. http://www.acreditclinic.com/pdf/library/quest-for-the-perfect-credit-score.pdf.

Mangla, Ismat Sarah. "The Quest for the Perfect Credit Score." *Money Magazine*. September 2010.

Matters, Craig. "A Lottery Where Everybody Wins." *Money Magazine*. December 2013.

"Minimum Payment Calculator." *Credit Card.Com*. Accessed June 4, 2015. http://www.creditcards.com/calculators/.

"7 Tips on Putting Your Dollars to Work…for You!." *FDIC Consumer News Winter 2008/2009 Special Edition: Managing Your Money in Good Times and Bad*. Accessed June 4, 2015. https://www.fdic.gov/consumers/consumer/news/cnwin0809/tips.html.

"Brief History of IRS." *IRS.gov*. Updated November 4, 2014. http://www.irs.gov/uac/Brief-History-of-IRS.

Risotto, Andrea. "How Borrowers Choose and Repay Payday Loans." *THE PEW CHARITABLE TRUSTS*. February 20, 2013. http://www.pewtrusts

.org/en/research-and-analysis/reports/2013/02/19/how-borrowers-choose-and-repay-payday-loans.

Chen, Tim. "American Household Credit Card Debt Statistics: 2015." *Nerdwallet* (blog). Accessed May 28, 2015. www.nerdwallet.com/blog/credit-card-data/average-credit-card-debt-household/.

"Auto Leasing Guide: The Art of the Deal". *Lease Guide*. Accessed June 4, 2015. http://www.leaseguide.com/.

"Leasing 101". *DMV.ORG*. Accessed June 4, 2015. http://www.dmv.org/how-to-guides/leasing.php.

"Personal Finance." *Reader's Digest*. May 2013. p72.

"Post Tagged authorized user." *Experian: A World of insight (blog)*. Accessed June 4, 2015. http://www.experian.com/blogs/ask-experian/tag/authorized-user/.

Phillip, Reed. "Calculate Your Own Car Lease Payment." *Edmunds.com*. December 10, 2014. http://www.edmunds.com/car-leasing/calculate-your-own-lease-payment.html.

"Protection for in-Home Purchases: The Cooling-Off Rule". *Federal Trade Commission: Consumer News*. Accessed June 4, 2015. http://www.consumer.ftc.gov/articles/0176-protections-home-purchases-cooling-rule.

"Driven To Disaster: Car-Title Lending and Its Impact on Consumers". *Center for Responsible Lending*. February 28, 2013. http://www.responsiblelending.org/other-consumer-loans/car-title-loans/research-analysis/driven-to-disaster.html.

Peters, Eric. "Don't Finance Your Used Car". *LewRockwell.com*. May 6, 2011. http://www.lewrockwell.com/2011/05/eric-peters/dont-finance-your-used-car/.

Dunn, Alan. "Top 20 Celebrities who have Filed Bankruptcy" *How to Save Money?.com*. April 28, 2011. http://www.howtosavemoney.com/top-20-celebrities-who-have-filed-bankruptcy/#.VXIUC8vbLmI.

Fisher, Luchina. "Burt Reynolds on His Money Woes". *ABC News.com*. August 18, 2011. http://abcnews.go.com/Entertainment/burt-reynolds-bottoms-florida-foreclosure/story?id=14324008.

"Serrano Introduces Bill to Encourage Savings". *Issues: Economy and Jobs, Financial Services, The Bronx (Press Release)*. August 1, 2013. http://serrano.house.gov/press-release/serrano-introduces-bill-encourage-savings.

Brain, Marshall. "How Pawnshops Work". *Howstuffworks*. Assessed June 15, 2015. http://money.howstuffworks.com/pawnshop.htm.

Brain, Marshall, and Roos, Dave. "How Stocks and the Stock Market Work." *Howstuffworks*. Accessed June 4, 2015. http://money.howstuffworks.com/personal-finance/financial-planning/stocks.htm.

"Annual Earnings of Young Adults." *NATIONAL CENTER FOR EDUCATION STATISTICS*. May 2015. http://nces.ed.gov/programs/coe/indicator_cba.asp.

Phillips, Michael M. "Would you Pay $103,000 for This Arizona Fixer-Upper?" *THE WALL STREET JOURNAL*. Updated January 3, 2009. http://m.us.wsj.com/articles/SB123093614987850083?mg=reno64-ws.

"Subprime mortgage crises." *Wikipedia*. Accessed June 9, 2015. http://en.wikipedia.org/wiki/Subprime_mortgage_crisis.

Rubin, Richard. "Egg Donor Loses Case Against IRS, Must Pay Taxes on Earnings." *Bloomberg Business*. January 22, 2015. http://www.bloomberg.com/news/articles/2015-01-22/egg-donor-loses-case-against-irs-must-pay-taxes-on-earnings.

Vaughn, Carol. "Former H&R Block owner jailed for ID theft." *Delmarva Daily Times*. January 22, 2015. http://www.delmarvanow.com/story/news/local/virginia/2015/01/22/former-hr-block-owner-jailed-theft/22155597/.

Little, Jeffery B, and Rhodes, Lucien. "Wall Street—How It Works." *Understanding Wall Street*. 5th ed. McGraw-Hill, 2010.

"Get your Blue Book Value then Price Your Next Car." *Kelly Blue Book*. Accessed June 9, 2015. http://www.kbb.com/chevrolet/impala-limited/2014-chevrolet-impala-limited/lt-sedan-4d/options/?vehicleid=390794&intent=trade-in-sell&mileage=27000.

U. S. Department of the Treasury. Internal Revenue Service. (2013). 1040A: *U.S. Individual Income Tax Return*. (Cat. No. 11327A). Washington, DC: U.S. Government Publishing Office.

U. S. Department of the Treasury. Internal Revenue Service. (2014). Publication 559: *Survivors, Executors and Administrators*. (Cat. No. 15047D). Retrieved from http://www.irs.gov/pub/irs-pdf/p559.pdf.

U. S. Department of the Treasury. Internal Revenue Service. (2014). Publication 525: *Taxable and Nontaxable Income*. (Cat. No. 15047D). Retrieved from http://www.irs.gov/pub/irs-pdf/p525.pdf.

U. S. Department of the Treasury. Internal Revenue Service. (2014). Publication 590-A: *Contributions to Individual Retirement Arrangements (IRA)*. (Cat. No. 66302J) Retrieved from http://www.irs.gov/pub/irs-pdf/p590a.pdf.

U. S. Department of the Treasury. Internal Revenue Service. (2013). *1040A Instructions*. (Cat. No. 12088U). Retrieved from http://www.irs.gov/pub/irs-pdf/i1040a.pdf.

Sandberg, Erica. "5 key federal laws help protect credit cardholdrs" *CreditCards. com*. Accessed 12/9/2013. http://www.creditcards.com/credit-card-news/5-key-laws-protect-credit-cardholders-1377.php.

Detweiler, Gerri. "Creditor Gets a Judgment Against You – Now What?" *Credit.Com (Blog)*. January 25, 2012. http://blog.credit.com/2012/01/creditor-gets-a-judgment-against-you-now-what-51696/.

"Get ahead of your estate planning." *CNN Money (Money Essentials)*. Accessed June 4, 2015. http://money.cnn.com/magazines/moneymag/money101/lesson21/

"Annual Inflation Adjustment for 2013." *IRS.gov*. IR-2013-4, January 11, 2013. http://www.irs.gov/uac/Newsroom/Annual-Inflation-Adjustments-for-2013.

Garber, Julie. "Pros and Cons of Revocable Living Trusts." *About* (Blog). Accessed June 4, 2015. http://wills.about.com/od/overviewoftrusts/a/prosoftrusts.htm.

"Disability Statistics." *Council for Disability Awareness*. July 2013. http://www.disabilitycanhappen.org/docs/disability_stats.pdf

Palmer, Kimberly. "Why you Probably Need More Disability Insurance." *U.S. News & World Report*. Accessed June 14, 2015. http://money.usnews.com/money/personal-finance/articles/2013/10/09/why-you-probably-need-more-disability-insurance.

Shell, Adam. "Is it just a pullback, coming correction or beginning of bear market?" *USA Today Money*. August 4, 2014. http://americasmarkets.usatoday.com/2014/08/04/is-it-just-a-pullback-coming-correction-or-beginning-of-bear-market/.

"Beta (finance)." *Wikipedia*. Accessed June 5, 2015. http://en.m.wikipedia.org/wiki/Beta_(finance).

"Dividend Yield" *Investopedia*. Accessed June 5, 2015. http://www.investopedia.com/terms/d/dividendyield.asp.

"Earnings Per Share." *Finance Formulas*. Accessed June 5, 2015. http://www.financeformulas.net/Earnings_Per_Share.html.

"P/E Ratio: Using The P/E Ratio." *INVESTOPEDIA*. Accessed June 5, 2015. http://www.investopedia.com/university/peratio/peratio2.asp.

"The Time Value of Money." *Calculatornet*. Accessed June 5, 2015. http://www.calculator.net/finance-calculator.html?ctype=endamount&ctargetamountv=1000000&cyearsv=5&cstartingprinciplev=0&cinterestratev=2&ccontributeamountv=1460&ciadditionat1=beginning&printit=0&x=69&y=23.

"Predatory Lending Resources." *FDIC*. Accessed June 5, 2015. https://www.fdic.gov/regulations/resources/bankers/.

"How to Save Money." *WikiHow*. Accessed June 6, 2015. http://m.wikihow.com/Save-Money.

"Edmunds.com TMV-True Market Value." *Edmunds.com*. Accessed June 5, 2015. http://www.edmunds.com/tmv.html

Reed, Phillip. "Edmunds.com TMV-True Market Value." *Edmunds.com*. Accessed June 5, 2015. http://www.edmunds.com/tmv.html

"Confessions of a Car Salesman." *Edmunds.com*. May 4, 2009. http://www.edmunds.com/car-buying/confessions-of-a-car-salesman.html

Reed, Phillip. "How to use Edmunds True Cost to Own." *Edmunds.com*. May 30, 2009. http://www.edmunds.com/car-buying/confessions-of-a-car-salesman.html.

"What's in my FICO Scores." *myFICO*. Accessed May 6, 2015. http://www.myfico.com/crediteducation/whatsinyourscore.aspx.

"Understanding Credit Card Interest." *INVESTOPEDIA*. Accessed June 5, 2015. http://www.investopedia.com/articles/01/061301.asp.

Williamson, Samuel. "Purchasing Power of Money in the United States from 1774 to Present." *MeasuringWorth*. Accessed June 6, 2015. http://www.measuringworth.com/ppowerus/.

"How to Manage Your Finances." *wikiHow*. Accessed June 6, 2015. http://m.wikihow.com/Manage-Your-Finances.

"Dividend Yield" *INVESTOPEDIA*. Accessed June 7, 2015. http://www.investopedia.com/terms/d/dividendyield.asp.

"What is the Average Car Depreciation Rate?" *CarsDirect*. November 8, 2013. http://www.carsdirect.com/auto-loans/what-is-the-average-car-depreciation-rate.

"What Score Does Everyone Start With?" *Savvy on Credit*. Accessed June 7, 2015. http://www.savvyoncredit.com/credit-score-everyone-start/.

"How to Lease a Car." *howstuffworks*. Accessed June 6, 2015. http://auto.howstuffworks.com/buying-selling/how-to-lease-a-car.htm

"Statute of Limitations on Debts-Collections, Debt Settlement, Debt Collection." *Credit Infocenter*. March 9, 2915. http://www.creditinfocenter.com/rebuild/statuteLimitations.shtml.

"How Now, Dow? What Moves The DJIA?" *INVESTOPEDIA*. Accessed June 7, 2015. http://www.investopedia.com/articles/02/082702.asp

"Stocks Basics Tutorial." *INVESTOPEDIA*. Accessed June 7, 2015. http://www.investopedia.com/university/stocks/.

Bragg, James. "HOW THE AUTO INDUSTRY HAS DISGUISED DEALER INCENTIVE DOLLARS AS DEALER COST DOLLARS BY MOVING THEM FROM MSRP/STICKER PRICE INTO THE INVOICE PRICE FOR OVER 18 YEARS." Accessed June 7, 2015. http://fightingchance.com/addon04.php?js=y.

Howard, Clark. "Tips to avoid student loan debt." *Clark Howard*. July 2, 2013. http://www.clarkhoward.com/ways-avoid-heavy-burden-student-loan-debt.

Schick, Kate. "An Introduction To Stock Market Indexes." *INVESTOPEDIA*. Accessed June 7, 2015. http://www.investopedia.com/articles/analyst/102501.asp.

"New York Stock Exchange." *Wikipedia*. Accessed June 7, 2015. http://en.m.wikipedia.org/wiki/New_York_Stock_Exchange.

"United States housing bubble." *Wikipedia*. Accessed June 7, 2015. http://en.m.wikipedia.org/wiki/United_States_housing_bubble#Subprime_mortgage_industry_collapse.

Tuman, Diane. "List of Closing Costs and Fees." *Zillow*. October 12, 2012. http://en.m.wikipedia.org/wiki/United_States_housing_bubble#Subprime_mortgage_industry_collapse.

"Up Front Mortgage Insurance Premium Changes for FHA Loans." *FHA.com*. Accessed June 7, 2015. https://www.fha.com/fha_article?id=137.

Suiter, Daniel R. "Termites in the United States: What and Where?" *Termites 101.ORG*. Accessed June 7, 2015. http://www.termites101.org/termite-basics/termites-by-region.

Christie, Les. "What the new mortgage rules mean for you." *CNNMoney*. Accessed June 7, 2015. http://money.cnn.com/2014/01/10/real_estate/mortgage-rules/.

"Dividend Reinvestment Plans (DRIPs)." *directinvesting.com*. Accessed June 7, 2015. http://www.directinvesting.com/drip_learning_center/what_are_drips.cfm.

Dratch, Dana. "10 most and least expensive cars to insure." *Bankrate*. Accessed January 6, 2013. http://www.bankrate.com/finance/insurance/10-most-and-least-expensive-cars-to-insure-1.aspx.

"Defined Benefit Plans versus Defined Contribution Plans." *My retirement paycheck*. Accessed June 7, 2015. http://www.myretirementpaycheck.org/retirement-plans/defined-benefit-plans.aspx.

Preston, Alyssa. "Predatory Payday Lending Its Effects and How to Stop It." *Center for American Progress*. August 20, 2013. https://www.americanprogress.org/issues/economy/report/2013/08/20/72591/predatory-payday-lending/

Soave, Robby. "It's Personal: Obamas carries $120,000 student loan debts for decades." *The Daily Caller*. August 27, 2013. http://dailycaller.com/2013/08/27/its-personal-obamas-carried-120000-student-loan-debt-for-decades/.

Calmes, Jackie. "Obama Plans Steps to Ease Student Debt." *The New York Times*. June 7, 2014. http://mobile.nytimes.com/2014/06/08/us/politics/obama-plans-steps-to-ease-student-debt.html?referrer=&_r=0.

"State taxes: Georgia." *Bankrate*. Accessed June 7, 2015. http://mobile.nytimes.com/2014/06/08/us/politics/obama-plans-steps-to-ease-student-debt.html?referrer=&_r=0.

Rayfield, Nicolas. "National student loan debt reaches a bonkers $1.2 trillion." *USA Today*. April 8, 2015. http://college.usatoday.com/2015/04/08/national-student-loan-debt-reaches-a-bonkers-1-2-trillion/.

Sandholm, Dean. "For Rubio, student loan bill is personal." *CNBC*. April 9, 2015. http://www.cnbc.com/id/101568230.

"What will your monthly mortgage payments be? Use this mortgage calculator." *Bankrate.com*. http://www.bankrate.com/partners/sem/mortgage-calculator-rates-tl.aspx?ec_id=m1027724&s_kwcid=AL!1325!3!41195874008!e!!g!!mortgage+calculator&ef_id=UYhHQgAABWTzu2iR%3a20140328204856%3as&MSA=0520&MSA=0520&MSA=0520&MSA=0520&MSA=0520&MSA=0520.

Hand, Mojo. "Charge-off." *Wikipedia*. Accessed June 7, 2015. http://en.m.wikipedia.org/wiki/Charge-off.

Simon, Jeremy M. "FICO reveals how common credit mistakes affect scores." *CreditCard.com*. Updated July 13, 2010. http://www.creditcards.com/credit-card-news/fico-credit-score-points-mistakes-1270.php.

Levin, Carl. "Wall Street and the financial crises: The role of investment banks (Sen. Carl Levin)." *The Hill* (blog). April 27, 2010. http://thehill.com/blogs/

congress-blog/campaign/94549-wall-street-and-the-financial-crisis-the-role-of-investment-banks-sen-carl-levin.

Jeffery B. Little and Lucien Rhodes. "Understanding Wall Street, Fifth Edition". *McGraw-Hill*, 2010.

Ashoka. "Banking The Underbanked: A How To" *Forbes.com*. June 14, 2013. http://www.forbes.com/sites/ashoka/2013/06/14/banking-the-unbanked-a-how-to/.

Clair. "Payday Loans a Tempting Danger For People of All Economic Backgrounds." *Ready for Zero.* (blog). October 10, 2013. http://blog.readyforzero.com/payday-loans-a-tempting-danger-for-people-of-all-economic-backgrounds/.

"Fresh Start Checking Accounts." *ChexInfo*. March 8, 2013. http://www.chexinfo.com/fresh-start-checking-accounts/.

Dixon, Patrick. "The Future of Outsourcing – Impact on Jobs – Keynote Speaker." *Global Change.com*. Accessed June 14, 2015. http://www.globalchange.com/outsourcing.htm.

"Understanding Deposit Insurance." *FDIC.gov*. Accessed June 14, 2015. https://www.fdic.gov/deposit/deposits/.

Bell, Charles. "Bank overdraft protection: Do you need it?" *Bankrate*. Accessed June 14, 2015. http://www.bankrate.com/finance/savings/bank-overdraft-protection-do-you-need-it-1.aspx.

Nico, Leyva. "Second Chance Checking: Real Information and Resources." *Nerdwallet* (blog). Accessed June 14, 2015. http://www.nerdwallet.com/blog/checking/second-chance-checking/.

Phillips, Lisa. "EWS can stop you from opening a bank account." *rebuild credit scores*. April 9, 2015. http://rebuildcreditscores.com/early-warning-services/.

"Ally Bank and ChexSystems Policy." *ChexInfo*. http://www.chexinfo.com/ally-bank-and-chexsystems-policy/.

Ramsey, Dave. "Get Out of Debt with the Debt Snowball Plan." *DAVE RAMSEY*. August 2009. http://www.daveramsey.com/blog/get-out-of-debt-with-the-debt-snowball-plan/.

Moneyseed, Johnny. "A Step-by-Step Guide to Getting Out of Debt." *lifehacker.* December 3, 2013. http://lifehacker.com/a-step-by-step-guide-to-getting-out-of-debt-1475515477.

"What's in a Mortgage Payment?" *home loan learning center.* Accessed June 14, 2015. http://www.homeloanlearningcenter.com/mortgagebasics/whatsinamortgagepayment.htm.

"Mortgage Types." *home loan learning center.* Accessed June 14, 2015. http://www.homeloanlearningcenter.com/MortgageBasics/MortgageTypes.htm.

"Statutes Enforced or Administered by the Commission." *Federal Trade Commission Protecting America's Consumers.* Accessed June 14, 2015. https://www.ftc.gov/enforcement/statutes.

Smith, Lisa. "5 Insurance Policies Everyone Should Have." *INVESTOPEDIA.* Accessed June 14, 2015. http://www.investopedia.com/articles/pf/07/five_policies.asp.

"Life Insurance: Types of life insurance policies." *CNN Money.* May 29, 2015. http://money.cnn.com/pf/money-essentials-life-insurance-policies/index.html.

"Vehicle Coverages." DMV.ORG. Accessed June 14, 2015. http://www.dmv.org/insurance/vehicle-coverages.php.

"Understanding Your FICO Score" *my FICO.* Accessed April 6, 2014. http://www.myfico.com/Downloads/Files/myFICO_UYFS_Booklet.pdf.

"Liability Insurance." DMV.ORG. Accessed June 14, 2015. http://www.dmv.org/insurance/liability-insurance.php.

"Medical Coverages." DMV.ORG. Accessed June 14, 2015. http://www.dmv.org/insurance/medical-coverages.php.

"Taxpayer Bill of Rights." *IRS.gov.* Accessed June 14, 2015. http://www.irs.gov/Taxpayer-Bill-of-Rights.

"Historical Documents relating to Alfonso (Al) Capone, Chicago." *IRS.gov.* Updated August 18, 2012. http://www.irs.gov/uac/Historical-Documents-relating-to-Alphonse-(Al)-Capone,-Chicago.

Clark, Josh. "Why was the tax evasion the only thing pinned on Al Capone?" *how stuff works*. Accessed June 14, 2015. http://history.howstuffworks.com/history-vs-myth/capone-tax-evasion.htm.

Garber, Julie. "Overview of Types of Property Ownership. *about money*. Accessed June 14, 2015. http://wills.about.com/od/ownershipofproperty/qt/propertysum.htm.

Garber, Julie. "The Latest in Wills & Estate Planning." *about money*. Accessed June 14, 2014. http://wills.about.com/.

Obringer, Lee Ann and Ross, Dave. "How Mortgages Work." *howstuff works*. http://home.howstuffworks.com/real-estate/buying-home/mortgage2.htm.

Simon, Jeremy M. "FICO reveals how common credit mistakes affect Scores Disclosed for the 1st time, 'damage points' taken off for late payments." *CreditCards.com*. Accessed June 14, 2015. http://www.creditcards.com/credit-card-news/fico-credit-score-points-mistakes-1270.php#ixzz2JUIGei8w.

Adams, Laura. "How to Raise Your Credit Score Fast." *QuickAndDirtyTips. com*. March 2, 2010. http://www.quickanddirtytips.com/money-finance/credit/how-to-raise-your-credit-score-fast.

Healey, James R, Woodyard, Chris, and Meier, Fred. "Suprising Tips For New-Car Buying In The Internet Age." *USA Today*. December 7, 2012. http://www.usatoday.com/story/money/cars/2012/12/06/car-shopping-prices-roundtable/1749101/.

"What is ChexSystem?" *ChexInfo*. January 25, 2013. http://www.chexinfo.com/what-is-chexsystem/.

Amadeo, Kimberly. "10-Year Treasury Note-How It works, Why It's the Most Important." *About News*. Accessed June 15, 2015. http://useconomy.about.com/od/fiscalpolicydefinitions/p/10-Year-Treasury.htm.

Amadeo, Kimberly. "What Is the Relationship Between Treasury Notes and Mortgage Rates?-Why Interest Rates Rise When the Economy Is Growing." *About News*. http://useconomy.about.com/od/economicindicators/f/Relationship Between Treasury Notes and Mortgage Rates.htm.

Risotto, Andrea. "How Borrowers Choose and Repay Payday Loans." *THE PEW CHARITABLE TRUSTS.* February 20, 2013. http://www.pewtrusts.org/en/research-and-analysis/reports/2013/02/19/how-borrowers-choose-and-repay-payday-loans.

Sullivan, Bob. "Pay $2,140 to borrow $950? That's how car title loans work." *NBC News.* March 5, 2013. http://business.nbcnews.com/_news/2014/03/18/23138986-pay-2140-to-borrow-950-thats-how-car-title-loans-work?lite.

"Car Leasing Terms Explained in Plain English." *REAL CAR TIPS.* Accessed June 15, 2015. http://www.realcartips.com/leasing/0050-auto-lease-terms.shtml.

Curry, Pat. "How a Supreme Court ruling killed off usury laws for credit card rates. Accessed November 12, 2013. *CreditCard.com.* http://www.creditcards.com/credit-card-news/marquette-interest-rate-usury-laws-credit-cards-1282.php.

Prater, Connie. "Issuer of 79.9% interest rate credit card defends its product." *CreditCards.com.* Accessed November 11, 2013. http://www.creditcards.com/credit-card-news/first-premier-79-rate-fees-credit-card-1265.php.

Reed, Phillip. "Calculate Your Own Car Lease Payment." *Edmunds.com.* Republished September 27, 2013. http://www.edmunds.com/car-leasing/calculate-your-own-lease-payment.html.

"Beware of ChexSystems Help Sites that are Scamming People." *ChexInfo.* June 24, 2013. http://www.chexinfo.com/beware-chexsystems-help-sites-scamming-people/.

INDEX

H

health insurance 73
home inspection 69
homeowners insurance 77

I

I Bonds 46
internet Scams 28
Investing 29, 30, 32, 34, 45
Investment banks 65
irrevocable trust 94

L

last will and testament 91
lease a vehicle 55
liability insurance 75
life insurance 78, 79, 80, 101
lottery 33

M

money market accounts 45
mortgage insurance premium 70

N

Nasdaq Composite Index 40
new credit 11, 20, 85

O

Online banking 6
overdraft charge 2
overdraft rules 4

P

pawnshop 25
payday loans xiv, 26, 27
payment history 9, 18, 19, 31
personal balance sheet 90

power of attorney 94
predatory lending xiii, 27, 28
probate 92
property ownership 95
purchase of a vehicle 47

R

renting 59, 71
Retirement Savings Contribution Credit
     85
revocable trust 93
Risky Mortgage Loans 64
Roth IRA 83, 85
rule of 72 33

S

saving 29
secured debt 22
Standard & Poors 39
statute of limitations 14
stock exchanges 38
Stock indexes 39
stock market 2, 34, 35, 36, 38, 40, 45,
     65
stocks 33, 34, 35, 36, 37, 38, 39, 40,
     42, 45
student-loan debt xv
subprime lender 12

T

taxes 41, 48, 56, 58, 60, 78, 84, 87, 88,
     89, 90, 92, 93, 94, 97, 98, 99,
     100
The Mortgage Crisis 65
traditional IRA 84

U

Unsecured debt 22

www.ingramcontent.com/pod-product-compliance
Lightning Source LLC
Chambersburg PA
CBHW021943170526
45157CB00003B/915